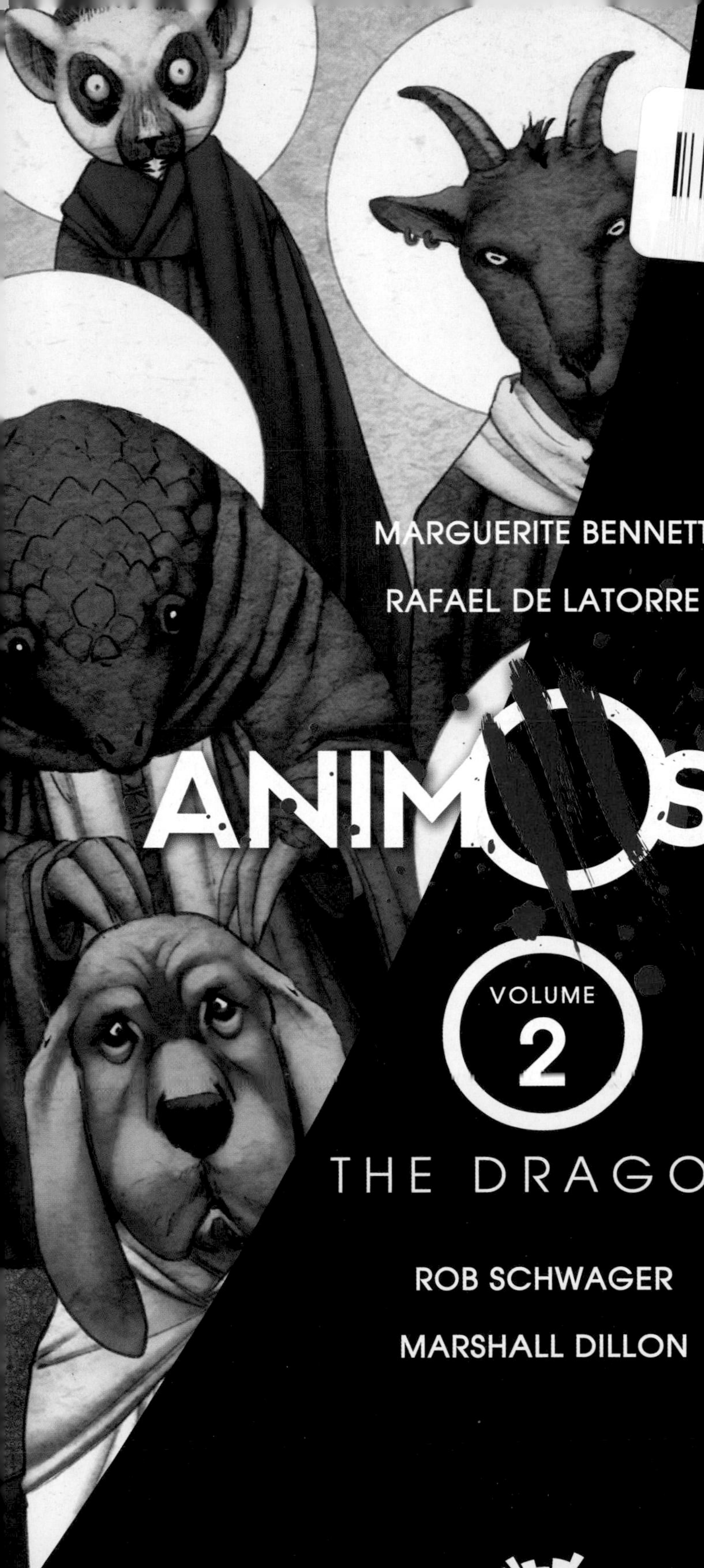



MARGUERITE BENNETT

RAFAEL DE LATORRE

# ANIMOSITY™

## VOLUME 2

## THE DRAGON

ROB SCHWAGER

MARSHALL DILLON

AFTERSHOCK™

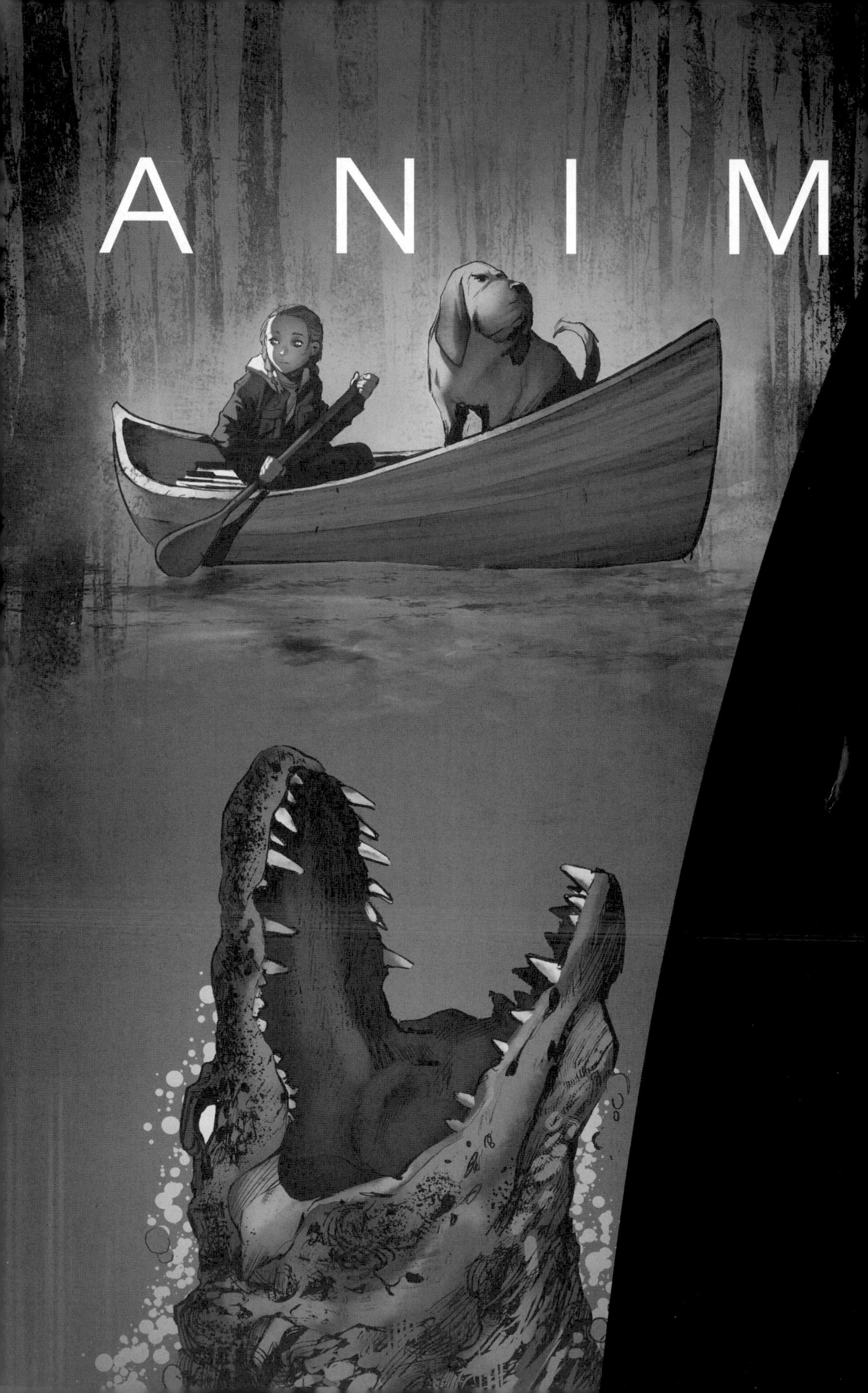
A N I M

OSITY
VOLUME 2
THE DRAGON

MARGUERITE BENNETT creator & writer

RAFAEL DE LATORRE artist

ROB SCHWAGER colorist

MARSHALL DILLON letterer

RAFAEL DE LATORRE w/ MARCELO MAIOLO front & original series covers

MIKE ROOTH NYCC variant cover & original series variant covers

KARL WALLER, ANDRE SZYMANOWICZ & COREY BREEN
World of Animosity art & design

JOHN J. HILL book & logo designer

MIKE MARTS editor

AFTERSHOCK™

MIKE MARTS - Editor-in-Chief • JOE PRUETT - Publisher/ Chief Creative Officer • LEE KRAMER - President
JAWAD QURESHI - SVP, Investor Relations • JON KRAMER - Chief Executive Officer • MIKE ZAGARI - SVP, Brand
JAY BEHLING - Chief Financial Officer • STEPHAN NILSON - Publishing Operations Manager
LISA Y. WU - Retailer/Fan Relations Manager • ASHLEY WYATT - Publishing Assistant

AfterShock Trade Dress and Interior Design by JOHN J. HILL • AfterShock Logo Design by COMICRAFT
Original series production (issues 5-8) by CHARLES PRITCHETT • Proofreading by DOCTOR Z.
Publicity: contact AARON MARION (aaron@fifteenminutes.com) & RYAN CROY (ryan@fifteenminutes.com) at 15 MINUTES
Special thanks to TEDDY LEO & LISA MOODY


First Printing: September 2017. 10 9 8 7 6 5 4 3 2 1

**AFTERSHOCKCOMICS.COM** Follow us on social media

# INTRODUCTION

Jesse and Sandor.

When my editor Mike Marts showed me the pitch for Animosity, I knew the relationship between these two characters would become something really special. And of course, who doesn't love the idea of animals becoming self-aware and seeking revenge on humans? Yes, I'd have to draw a lot of different animals, and that was definitely going to be a challenge for me, but there's no way I could pass on the opportunity to help create this story. Now I get to tell people that my job consists of drawing tortoises with rocket launchers strapped to their backs and angry goats wearing jackets. That's pretty neat.

Don't get me wrong, making comics is hard work. But it's so satisfying when you get to work with a talented writer like Marguerite. I really don't know what to expect when a new script arrives. Every issue is filled with so much emotion, humor, violence and love. The experience of bringing this world to life on the pages of a comic is even better when you work with such an amazing team. What a privilege it is to have Rob's gorgeous colors and Marshall's terrific lettering over the pages I've drawn, not to mention the stunning colors Maiolo has done for the covers. And of course, the work and support from the entire AfterShock crew.

But even with all the work we put into this comic book, it's only complete when you read it. Part of the story is told between the gutters, and it's a unique experience for each reader. I think it's the meaning you add and how you relate to the characters and the story itself that makes this series such a special experience. So thank you for joining us on this journey.

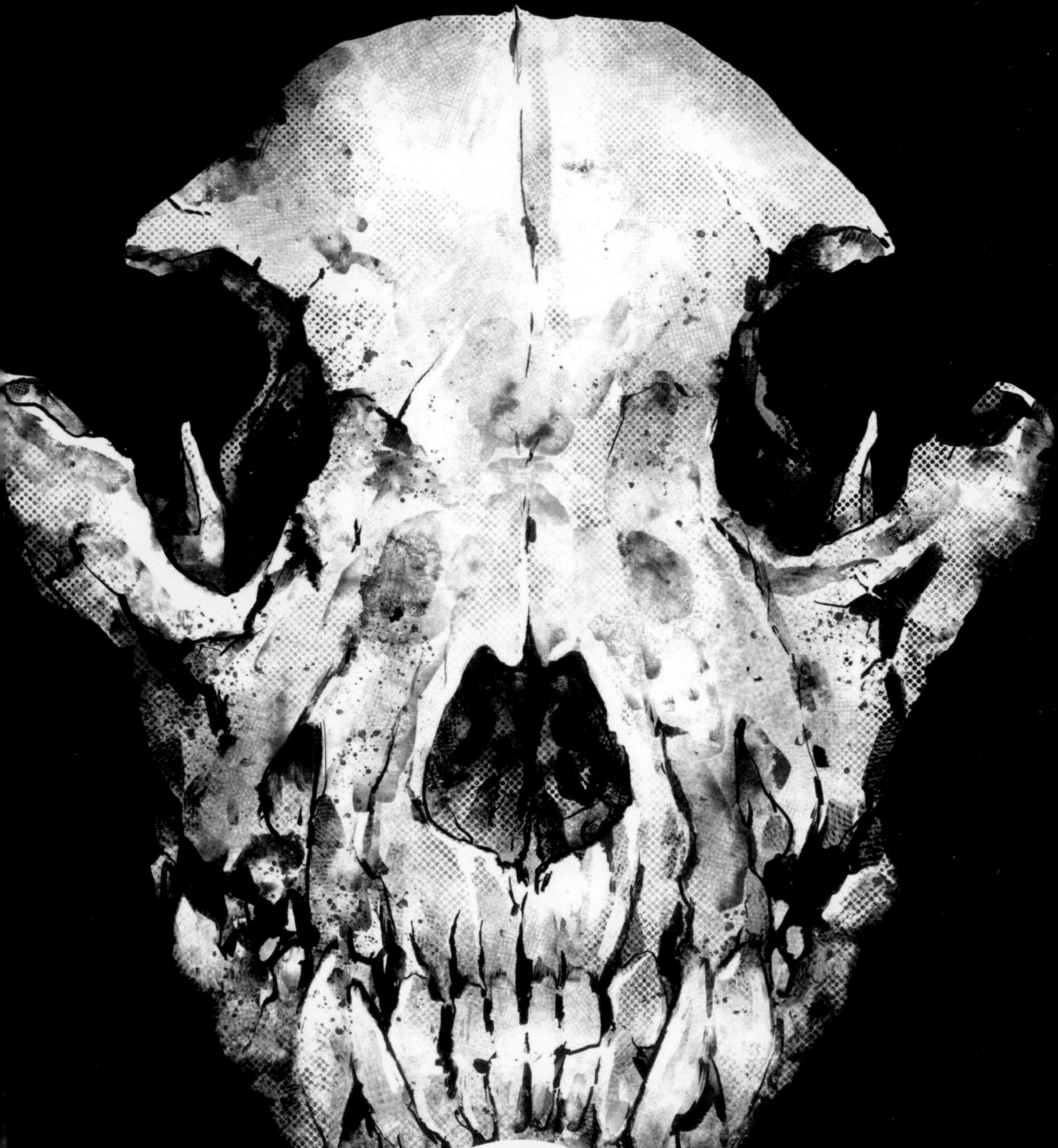

# 5

# "HERE THERE BE DRAGONS"

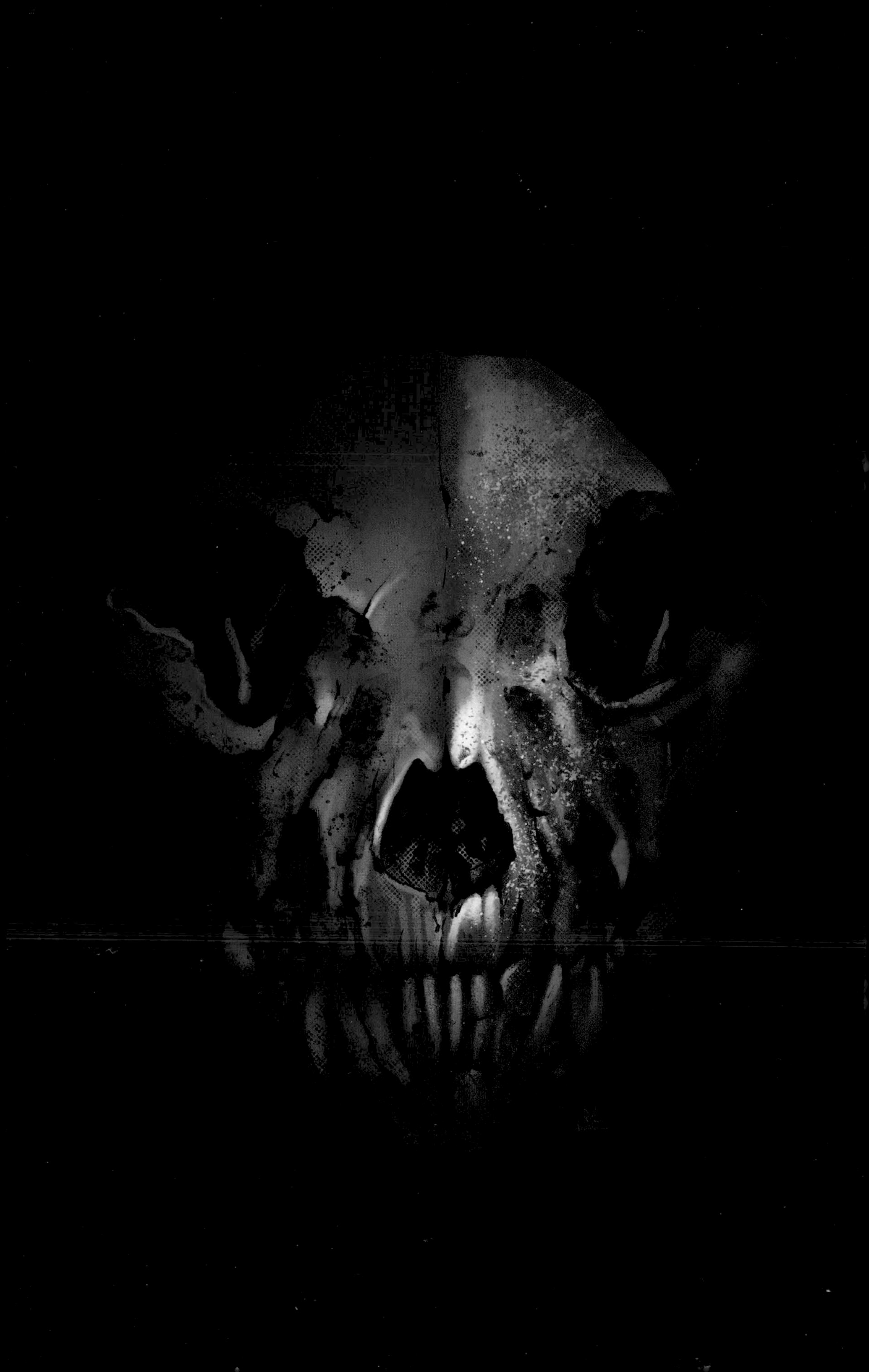

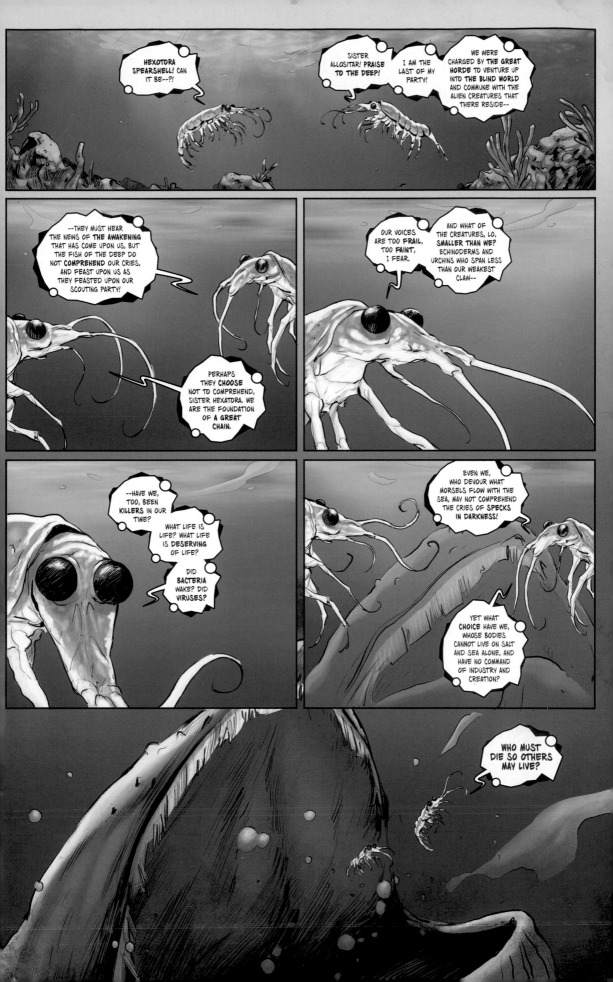

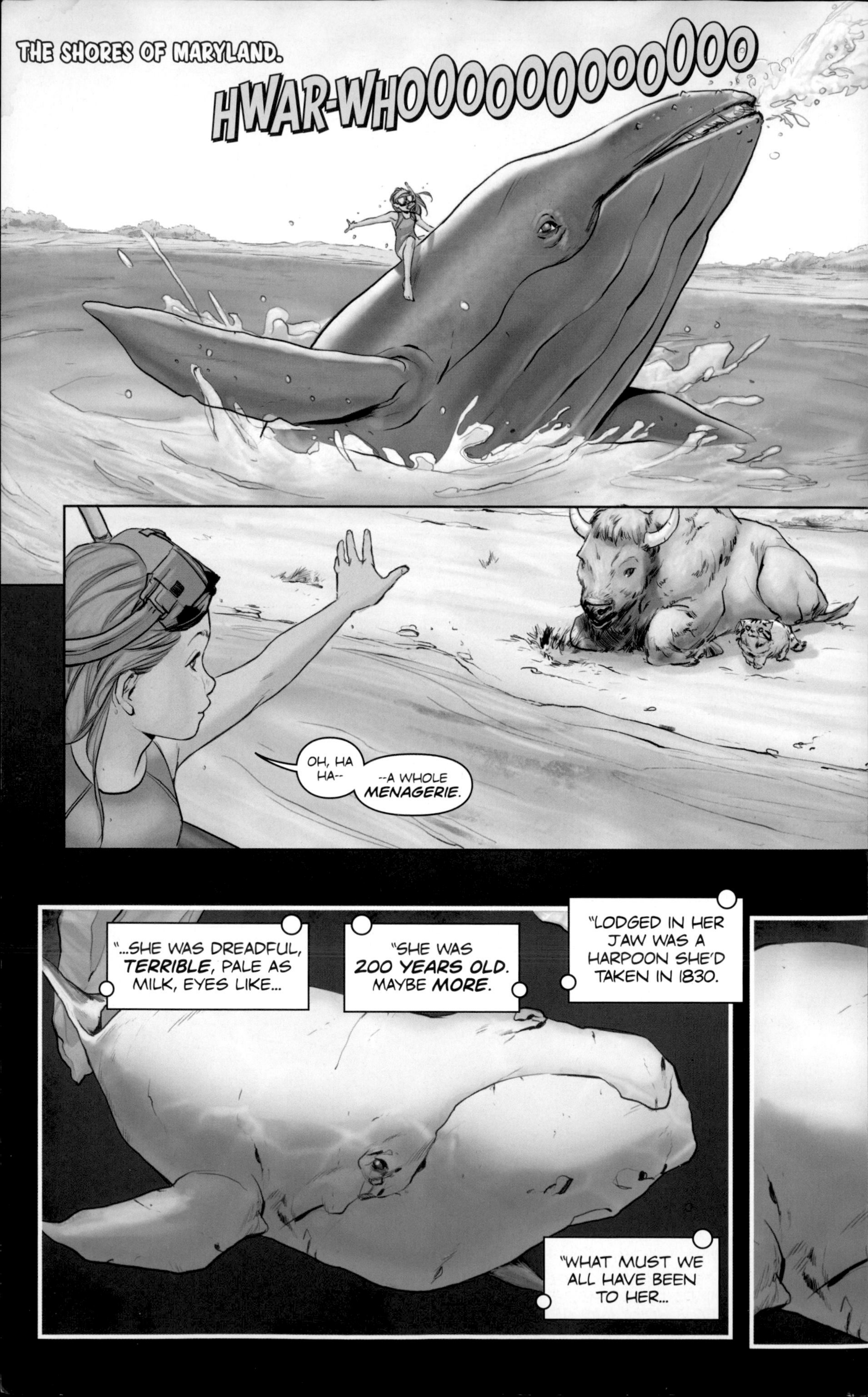
THE SHORES OF MARYLAND.
HWAR-WHOOOOOOOOOOOO
OH, HA HA--
--A WHOLE MENAGERIE.
"...SHE WAS DREADFUL, TERRIBLE, PALE AS MILK, EYES LIKE...
"SHE WAS 200 YEARS OLD. MAYBE MORE.
"LODGED IN HER JAW WAS A HARPOON SHE'D TAKEN IN 1830.
"WHAT MUST WE ALL HAVE BEEN TO HER...

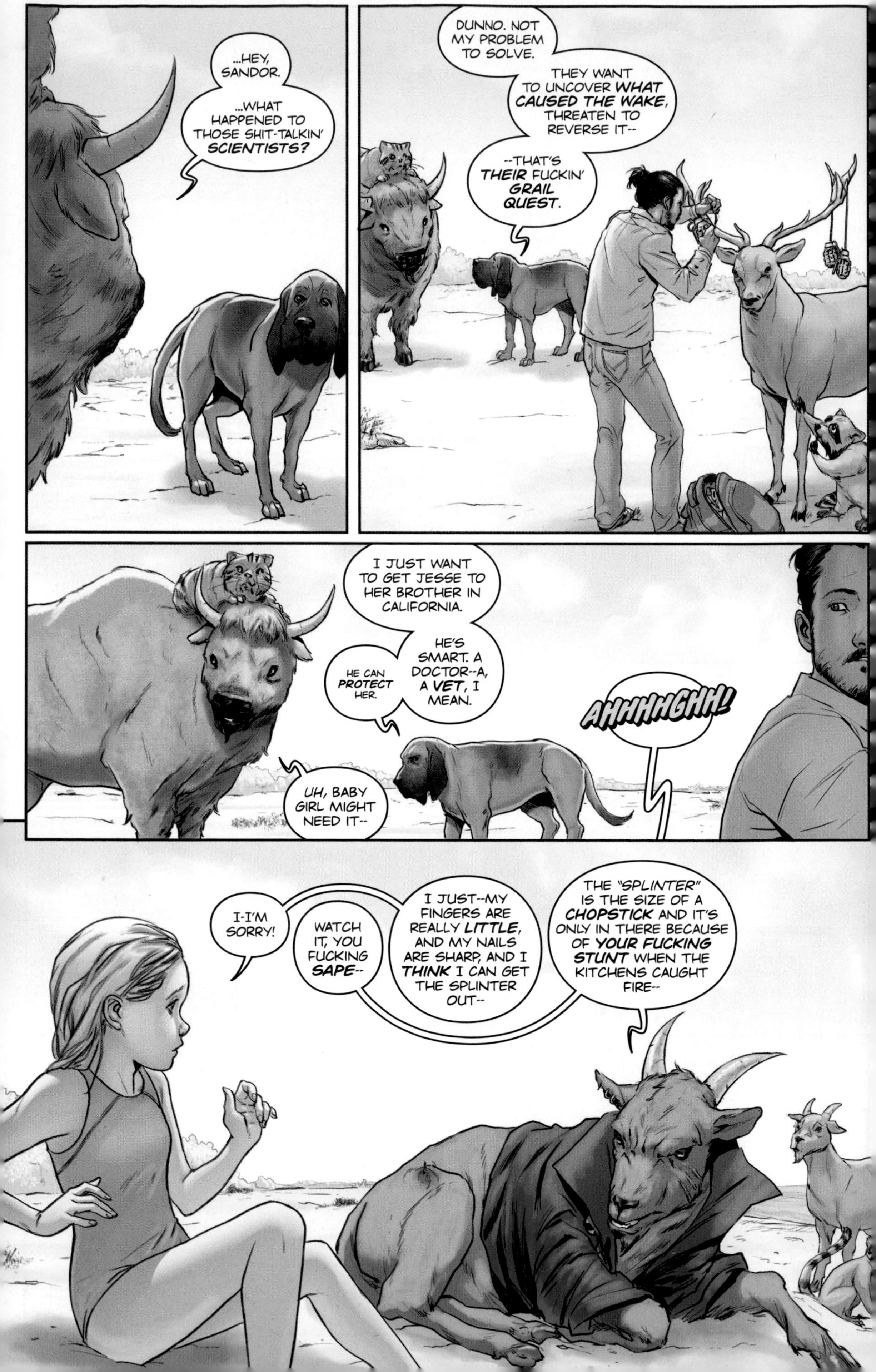
...HEY, SANDOR.
...WHAT HAPPENED TO THOSE SHIT-TALKIN' SCIENTISTS?
DUNNO. NOT MY PROBLEM TO SOLVE.
THEY WANT TO UNCOVER WHAT CAUSED THE WAKE, THREATEN TO REVERSE IT--
--THAT'S THEIR FUCKIN' GRAIL QUEST.
I JUST WANT TO GET JESSE TO HER BROTHER IN CALIFORNIA.
HE'S SMART. A DOCTOR--A, A VET, I MEAN.
HE CAN PROTECT HER.
UH, BABY GIRL MIGHT NEED IT--
AHHHHGHH!
I-I'M SORRY!
WATCH IT, YOU FUCKING SAPE--
I JUST--MY FINGERS ARE REALLY LITTLE, AND MY NAILS ARE SHARP, AND I THINK I CAN GET THE SPLINTER OUT--
THE "SPLINTER" IS THE SIZE OF A CHOPSTICK AND IT'S ONLY IN THERE BECAUSE OF YOUR FUCKING STUNT WHEN THE KITCHENS CAUGHT FIRE--

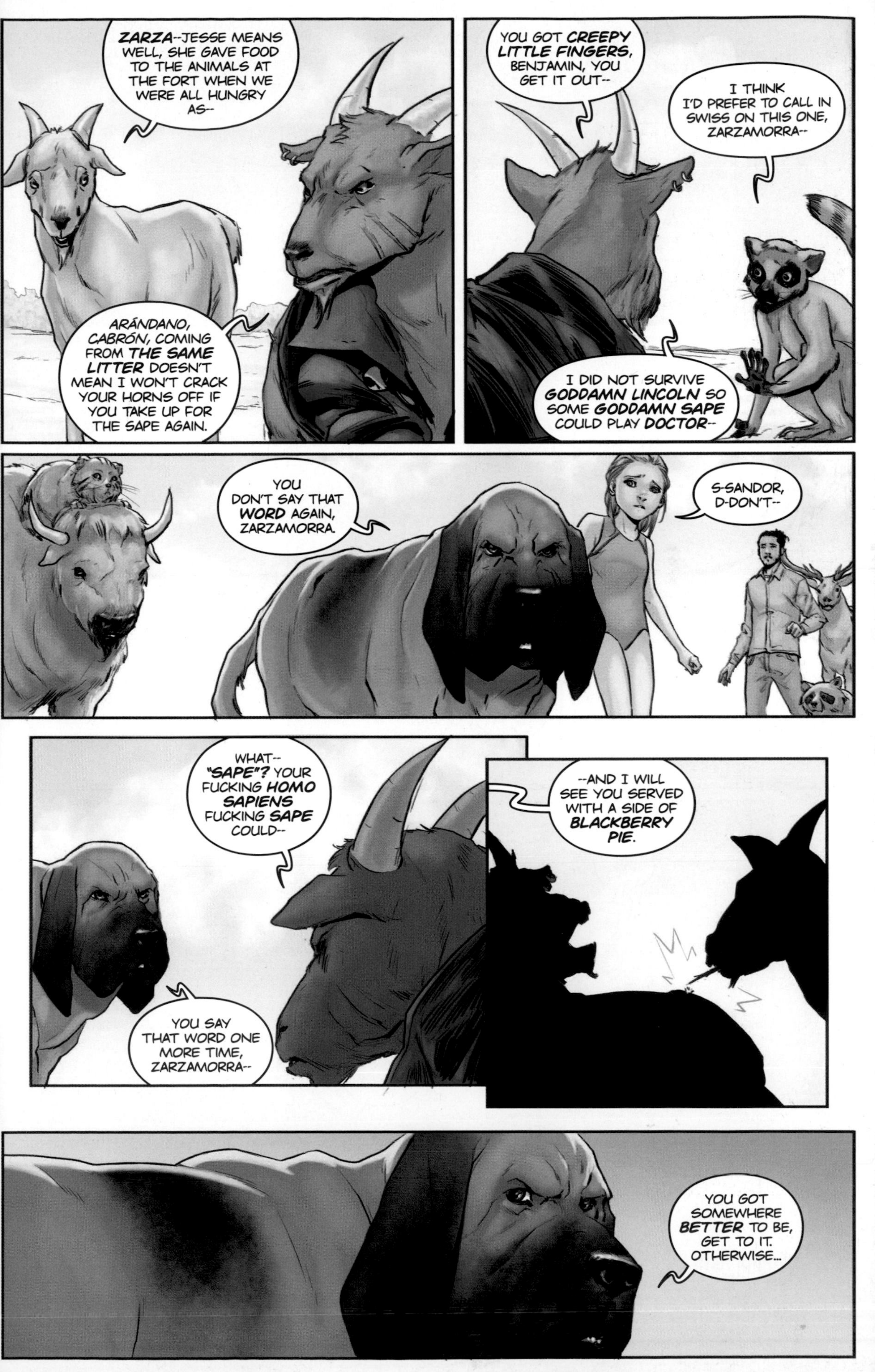

ZARZA--JESSE MEANS WELL, SHE GAVE FOOD TO THE ANIMALS AT THE FORT WHEN WE WERE ALL HUNGRY AS--
ARÁNDANO, CABRÓN, COMING FROM THE SAME LITTER DOESN'T MEAN I WON'T CRACK YOUR HORNS OFF IF YOU TAKE UP FOR THE SAPE AGAIN.
YOU GOT CREEPY LITTLE FINGERS, BENJAMIN, YOU GET IT OUT--
I THINK I'D PREFER TO CALL IN SWISS ON THIS ONE, ZARZAMORRA--
I DID NOT SURVIVE GODDAMN LINCOLN SO SOME GODDAMN SAPE COULD PLAY DOCTOR--
YOU DON'T SAY THAT WORD AGAIN, ZARZAMORRA.
S-SANDOR, D-DON'T--
WHAT-- "SAPE"? YOUR FUCKING HOMO SAPIENS FUCKING SAPE COULD--
YOU SAY THAT WORD ONE MORE TIME, ZARZAMORRA--
--AND I WILL SEE YOU SERVED WITH A SIDE OF BLACKBERRY PIE.
YOU GOT SOMEWHERE BETTER TO BE, GET TO IT. OTHERWISE...

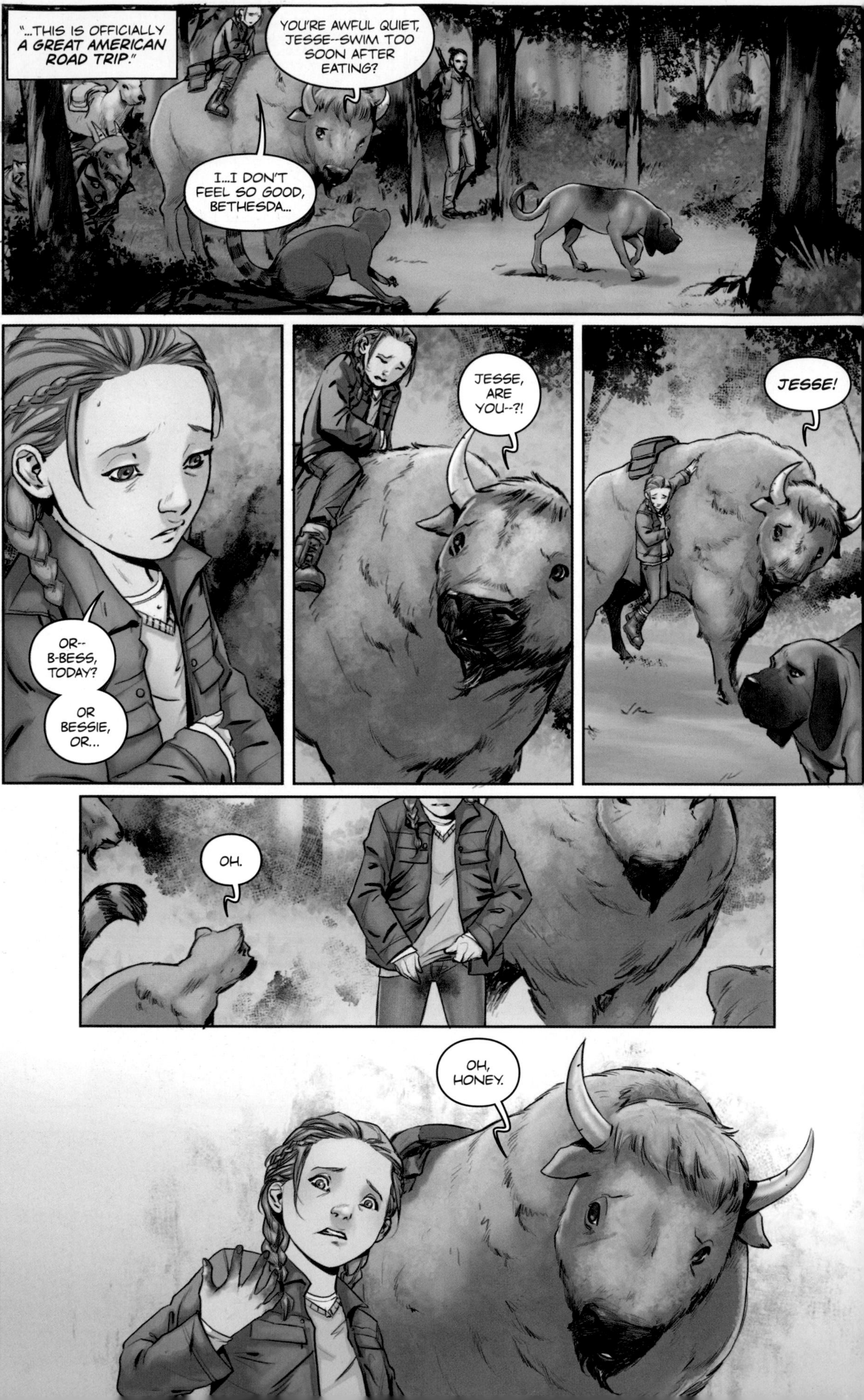
"...THIS IS OFFICIALLY *A GREAT AMERICAN ROAD TRIP*."
YOU'RE AWFUL QUIET, JESSE--SWIM TOO SOON AFTER EATING?
I...I DON'T FEEL SO GOOD, BETHESDA...
OR-- B-BESS, TODAY?
OR BESSIE, OR...
JESSE, ARE YOU--?!
JESSE!
OH.
OH, HONEY.

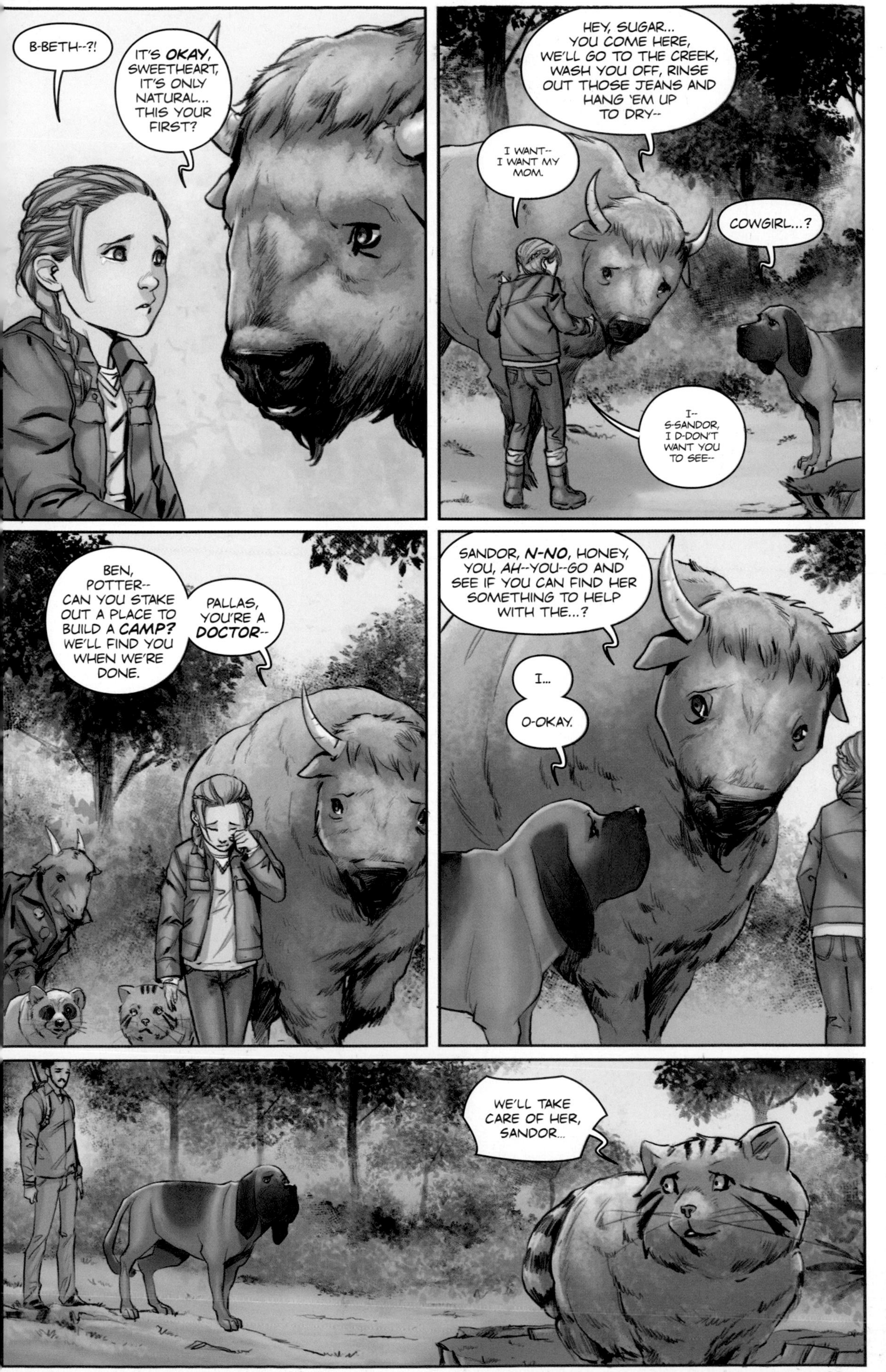
B-BETH--?!
IT'S **OKAY**, SWEETHEART, IT'S ONLY NATURAL... THIS YOUR FIRST?
HEY, SUGAR... YOU COME HERE, WE'LL GO TO THE CREEK, WASH YOU OFF, RINSE OUT THOSE JEANS AND HANG 'EM UP TO DRY--
I WANT-- I WANT MY MOM.
COWGIRL...?
I-- S-SANDOR, I D-DON'T WANT YOU TO SEE--
BEN, POTTER-- CAN YOU STAKE OUT A PLACE TO BUILD A **CAMP?** WE'LL FIND YOU WHEN WE'RE DONE.
PALLAS, YOU'RE A **DOCTOR**--
SANDOR, **N-NO**, HONEY, YOU, *AH*--YOU--GO AND SEE IF YOU CAN FIND HER SOMETHING TO HELP WITH THE...?
I...
O-OKAY.
WE'LL TAKE CARE OF HER, SANDOR...

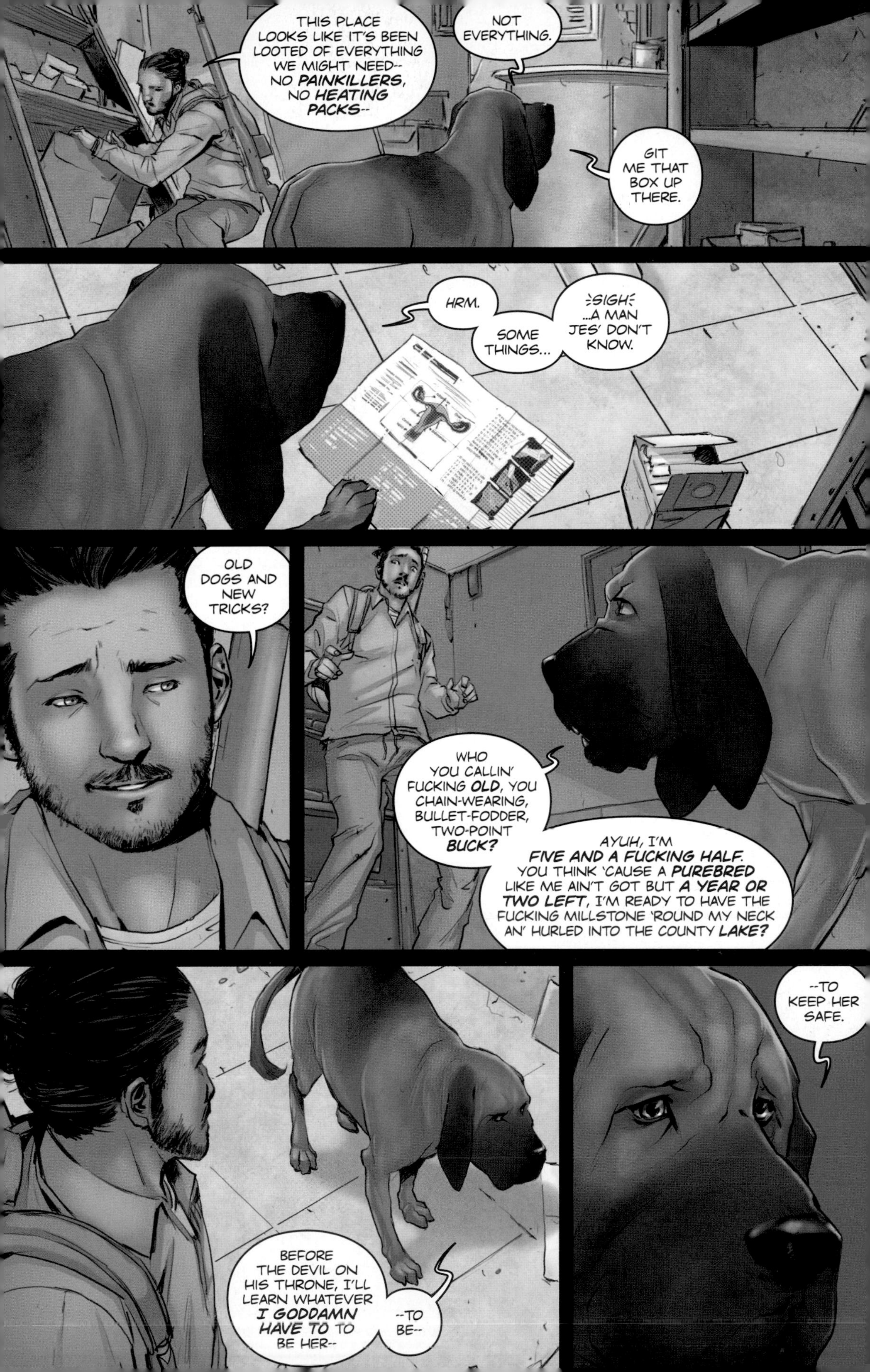
THIS PLACE LOOKS LIKE IT'S BEEN LOOTED OF EVERYTHING WE MIGHT NEED-- NO PAINKILLERS, NO HEATING PACKS--
NOT EVERYTHING.
GIT ME THAT BOX UP THERE.
HRM.
SOME THINGS...
SIGH ...A MAN JES' DON'T KNOW.
OLD DOGS AND NEW TRICKS?
WHO YOU CALLIN' FUCKING OLD, YOU CHAIN-WEARING, BULLET-FODDER, TWO-POINT BUCK?
AYUH, I'M FIVE AND A FUCKING HALF. YOU THINK 'CAUSE A PUREBRED LIKE ME AIN'T GOT BUT A YEAR OR TWO LEFT, I'M READY TO HAVE THE FUCKING MILLSTONE 'ROUND MY NECK AN' HURLED INTO THE COUNTY LAKE?
BEFORE THE DEVIL ON HIS THRONE, I'LL LEARN WHATEVER I GODDAMN HAVE TO TO BE HER--
--TO BE--
--TO KEEP HER SAFE.

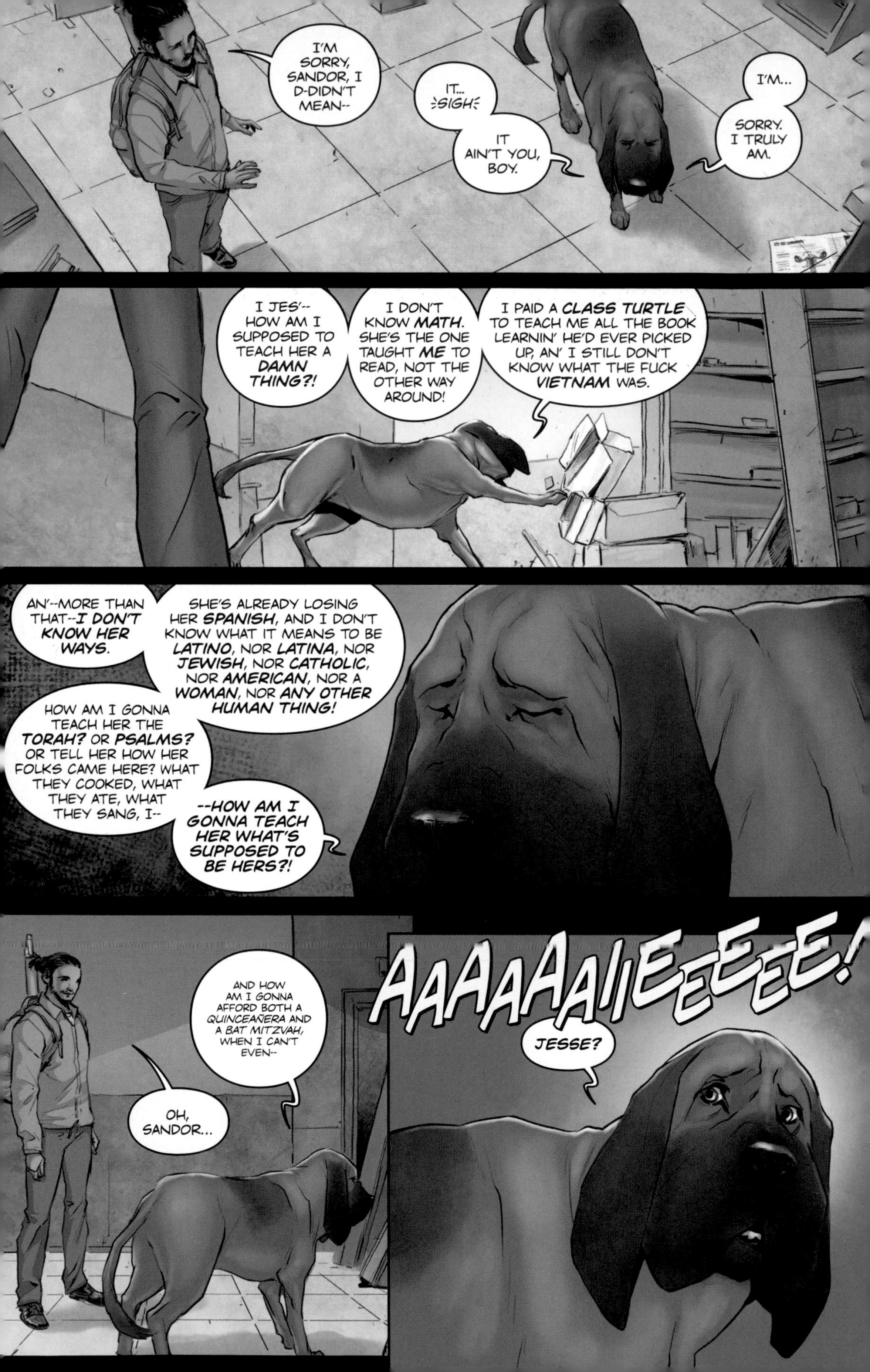

I'M SORRY, SANDOR, I D-DIDN'T MEAN--
IT... *SIGH*
IT AIN'T YOU, BOY.
I'M...
SORRY. I TRULY AM.
I JES'-- HOW AM I SUPPOSED TO TEACH HER A DAMN THING?!
I DON'T KNOW MATH. SHE'S THE ONE TAUGHT ME TO READ, NOT THE OTHER WAY AROUND!
I PAID A CLASS TURTLE TO TEACH ME ALL THE BOOK LEARNIN' HE'D EVER PICKED UP, AN' I STILL DON'T KNOW WHAT THE FUCK VIETNAM WAS.
AN'--MORE THAN THAT--I DON'T KNOW HER WAYS.
SHE'S ALREADY LOSING HER SPANISH, AND I DON'T KNOW WHAT IT MEANS TO BE LATINO, NOR LATINA, NOR JEWISH, NOR CATHOLIC, NOR AMERICAN, NOR A WOMAN, NOR ANY OTHER HUMAN THING!
HOW AM I GONNA TEACH HER THE TORAH? OR PSALMS? OR TELL HER HOW HER FOLKS CAME HERE? WHAT THEY COOKED, WHAT THEY ATE, WHAT THEY SANG, I--
--HOW AM I GONNA TEACH HER WHAT'S SUPPOSED TO BE HERS?!
AND HOW AM I GONNA AFFORD BOTH A QUINCEAÑERA AND A BAT MITZVAH, WHEN I CAN'T EVEN--
OH, SANDOR...
AAAAAAIIEEEEEE!
JESSE?

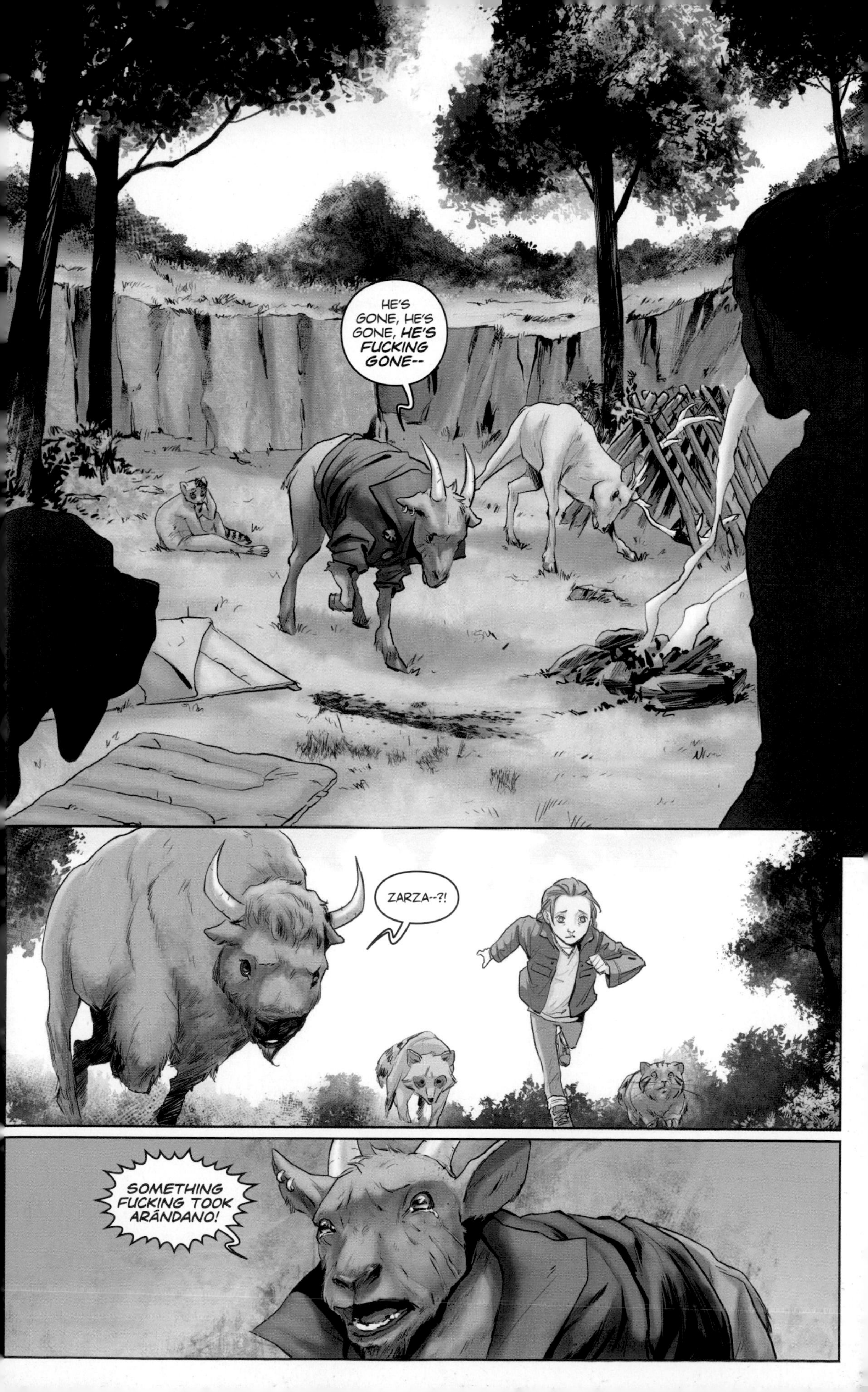
HE'S GONE, HE'S GONE, **HE'S FUCKING GONE--**
ZARZA--?!
SOMETHING FUCKING TOOK ARÁNDANO!

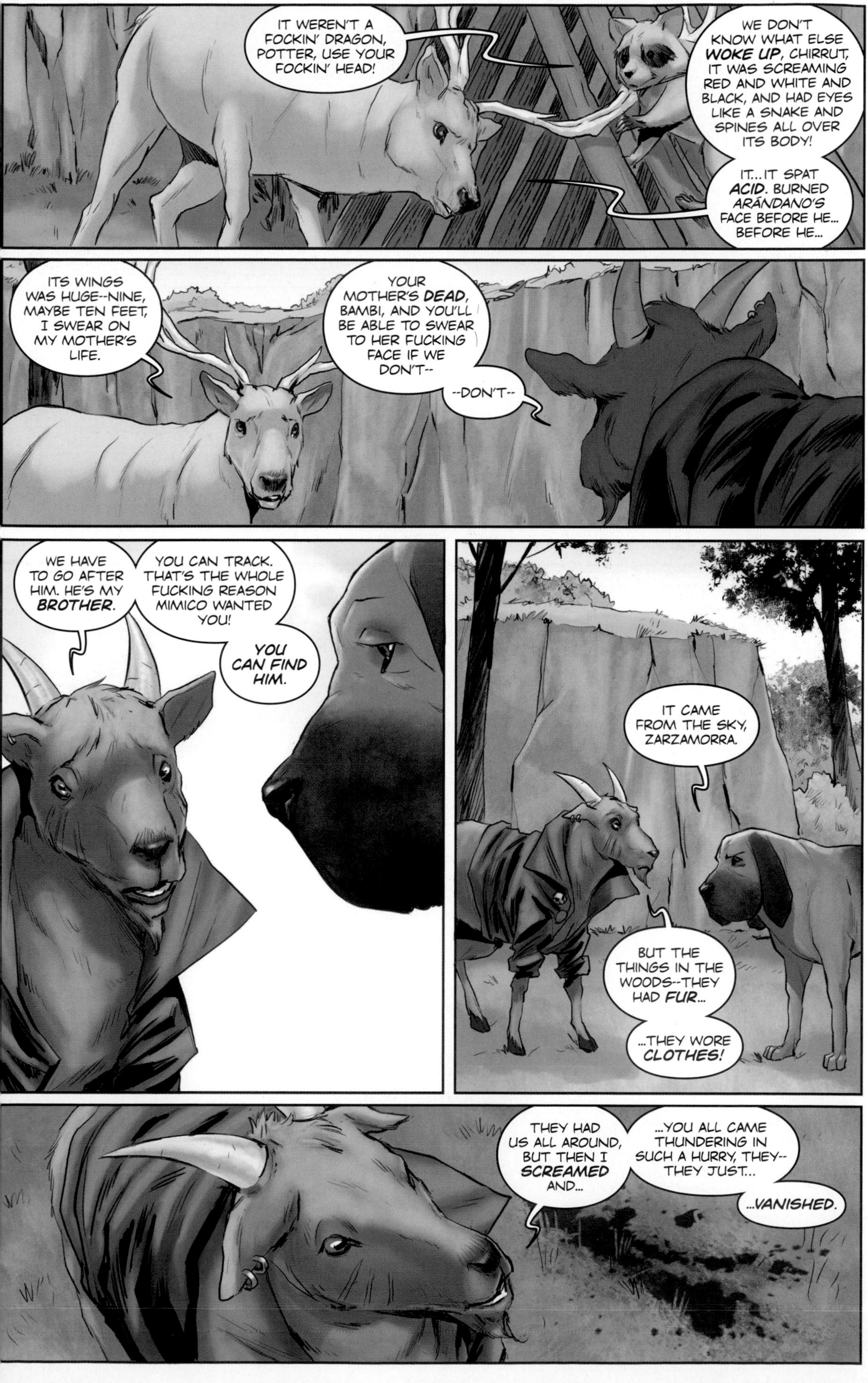
IT WEREN'T A FOCKIN' DRAGON, POTTER, USE YOUR FOCKIN' HEAD!
WE DON'T KNOW WHAT ELSE **WOKE UP**, CHIRRUT, IT WAS SCREAMING RED AND WHITE AND BLACK, AND HAD EYES LIKE A SNAKE AND SPINES ALL OVER ITS BODY!
IT... IT SPAT **ACID**. BURNED ARÁNDANO'S FACE BEFORE HE... BEFORE HE...
ITS WINGS WAS HUGE--NINE, MAYBE TEN FEET, I SWEAR ON MY MOTHER'S LIFE.
YOUR MOTHER'S **DEAD**, BAMBI, AND YOU'LL BE ABLE TO SWEAR TO HER FUCKING FACE IF WE DON'T--
--DON'T--
WE HAVE TO GO AFTER HIM. HE'S MY **BROTHER**.
YOU CAN TRACK. THAT'S THE WHOLE FUCKING REASON MIMICO WANTED YOU!
**YOU CAN FIND HIM.**
IT CAME FROM THE SKY, ZARZAMORRA.
BUT THE THINGS IN THE WOODS--THEY HAD **FUR**...
...THEY WORE **CLOTHES!**
THEY HAD US ALL AROUND, BUT THEN I **SCREAMED** AND...
...YOU ALL CAME THUNDERING IN SUCH A HURRY, THEY--THEY JUST...
...**VANISHED**.

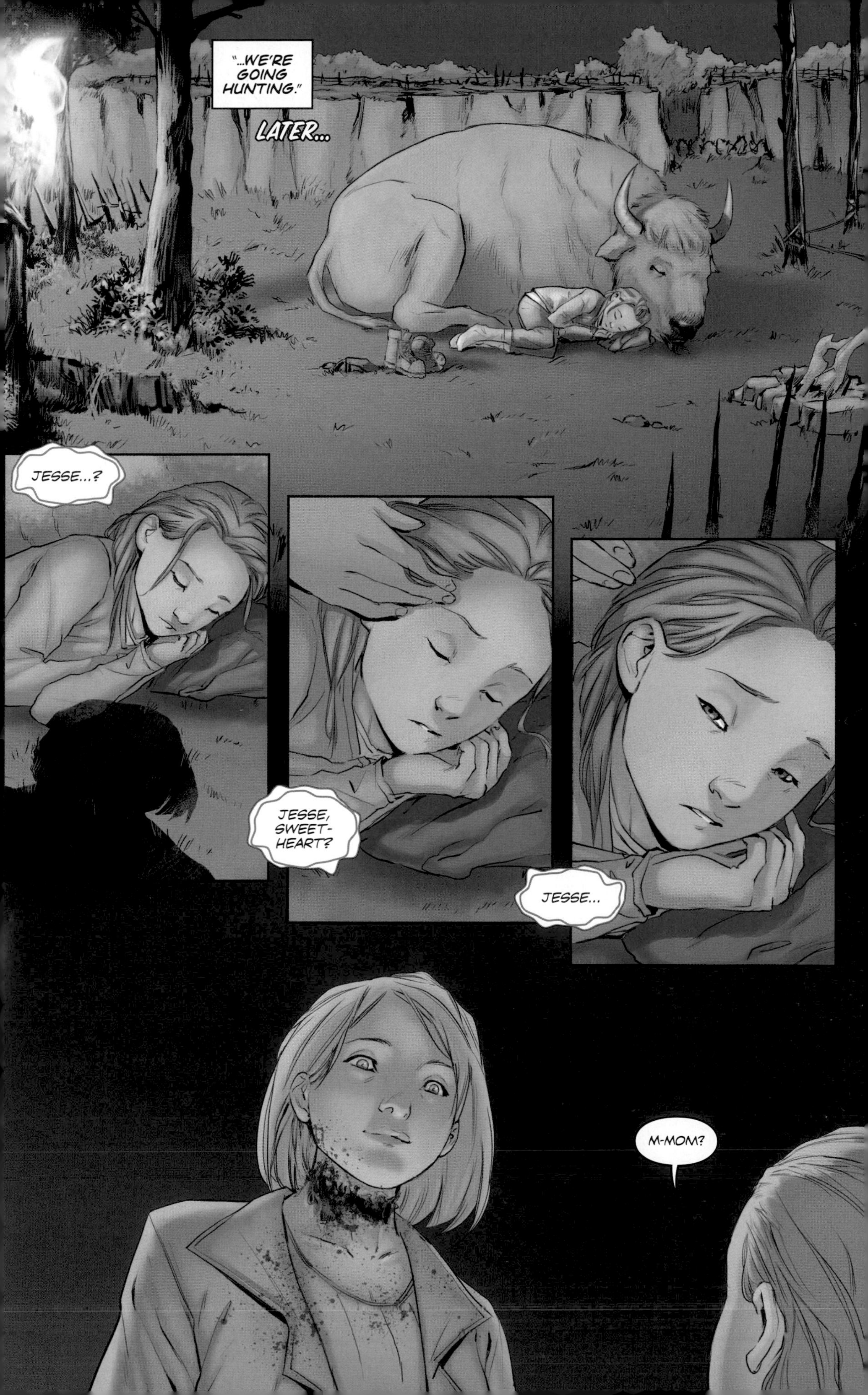
"...WE'RE GOING HUNTING."
LATER...
JESSE...?
JESSE, SWEET-HEART?
JESSE...
M-MOM?

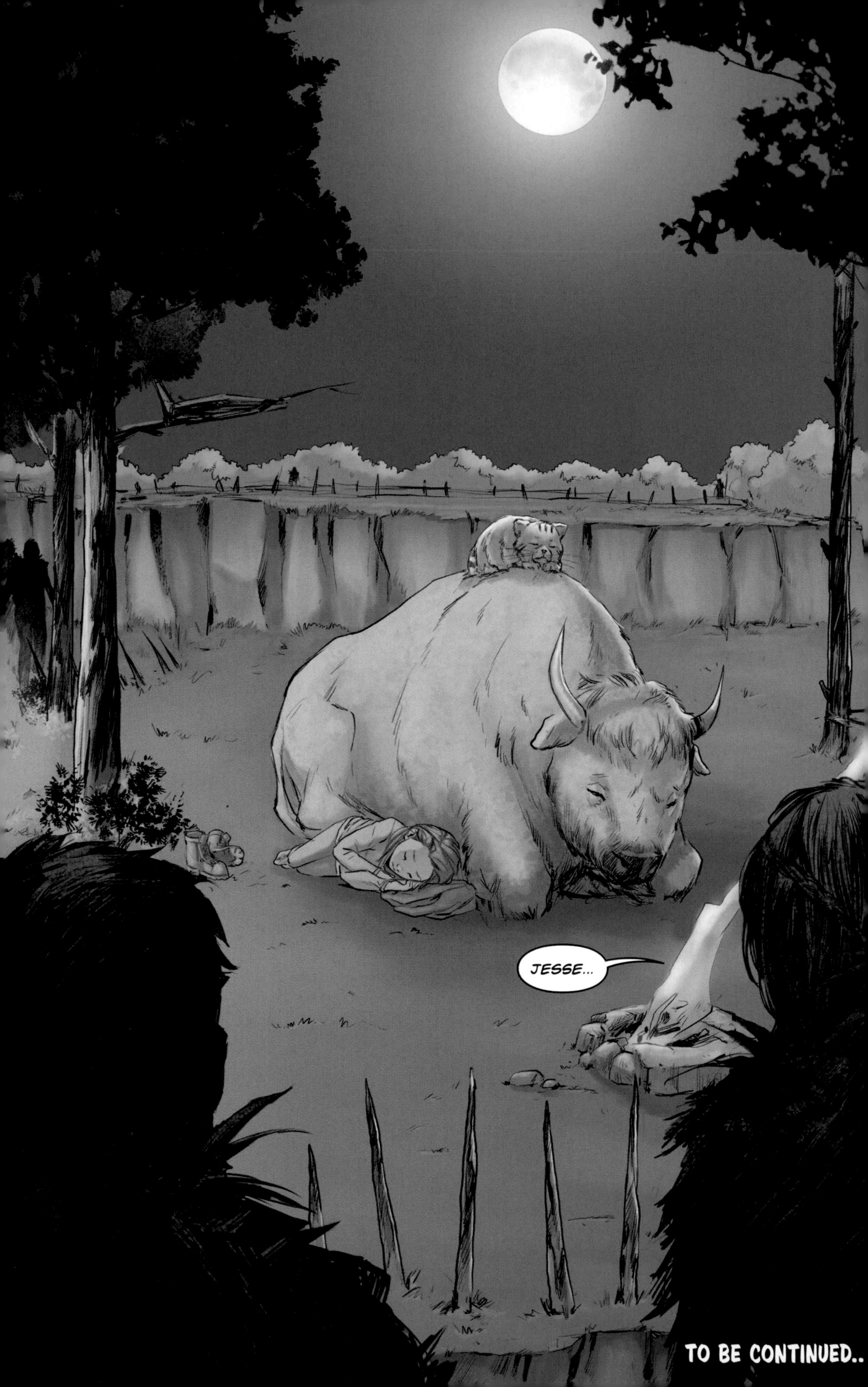
JESSE...
TO BE CONTINUED..

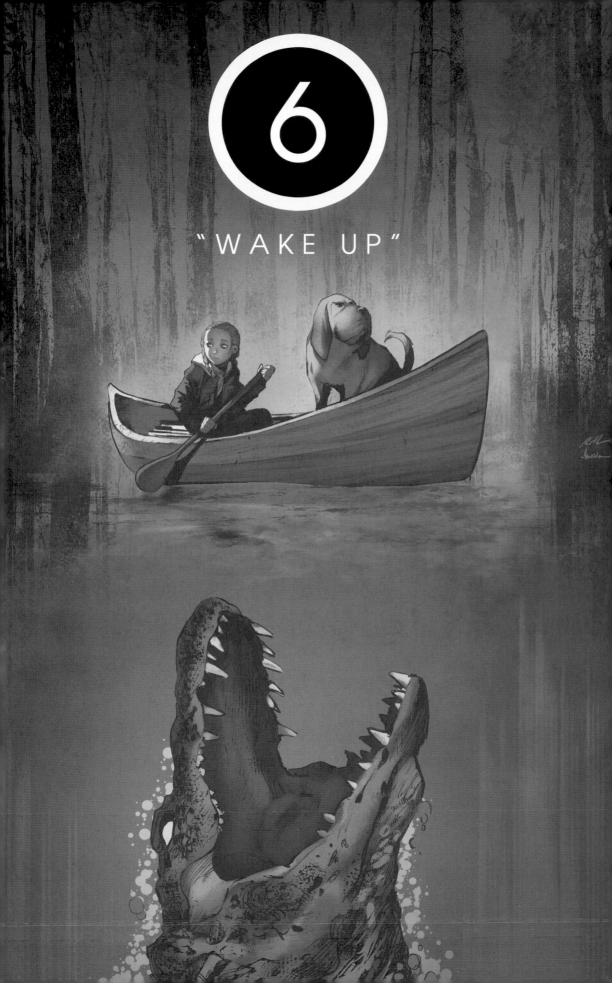

# 6

## "WAKE UP"

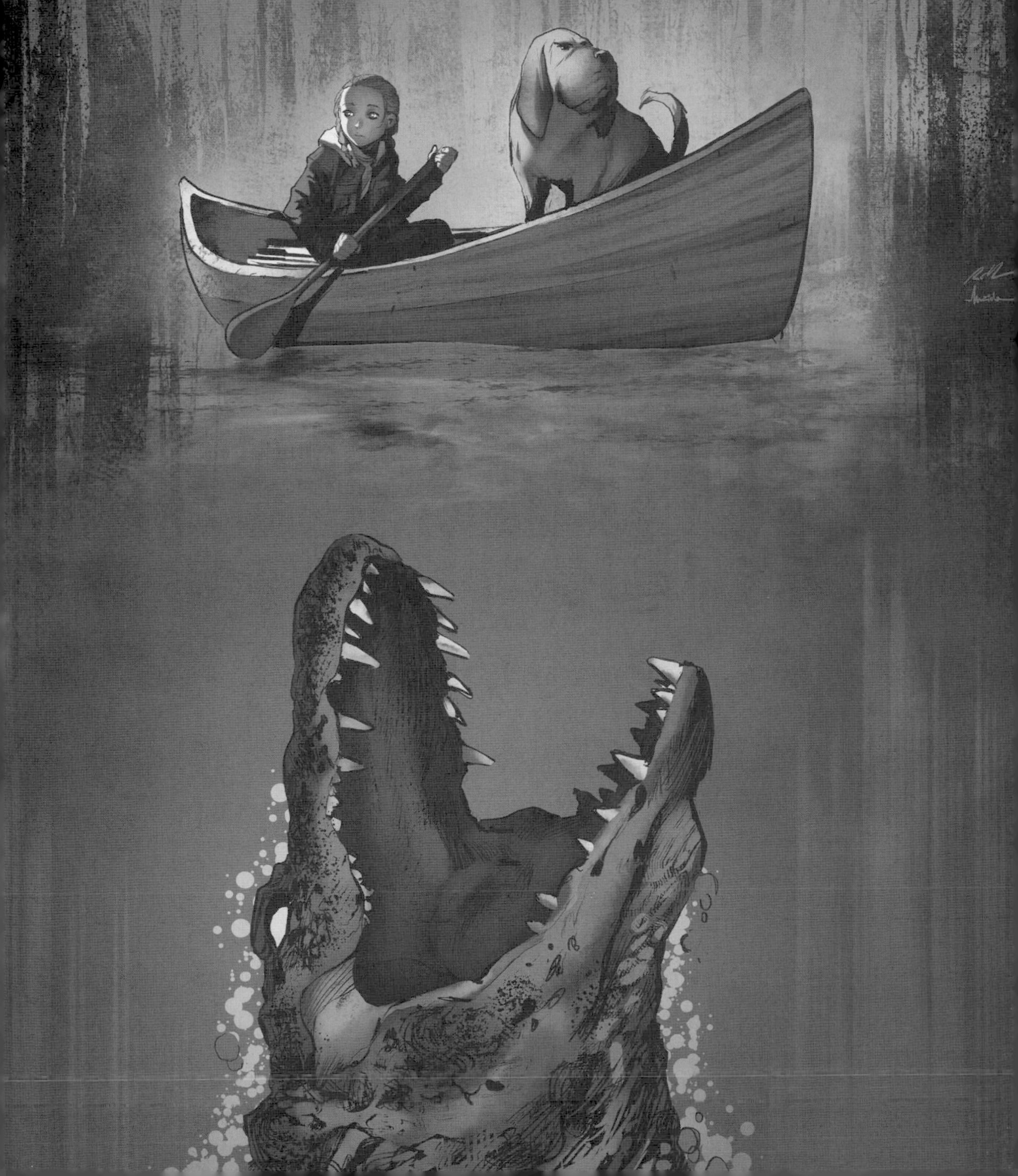

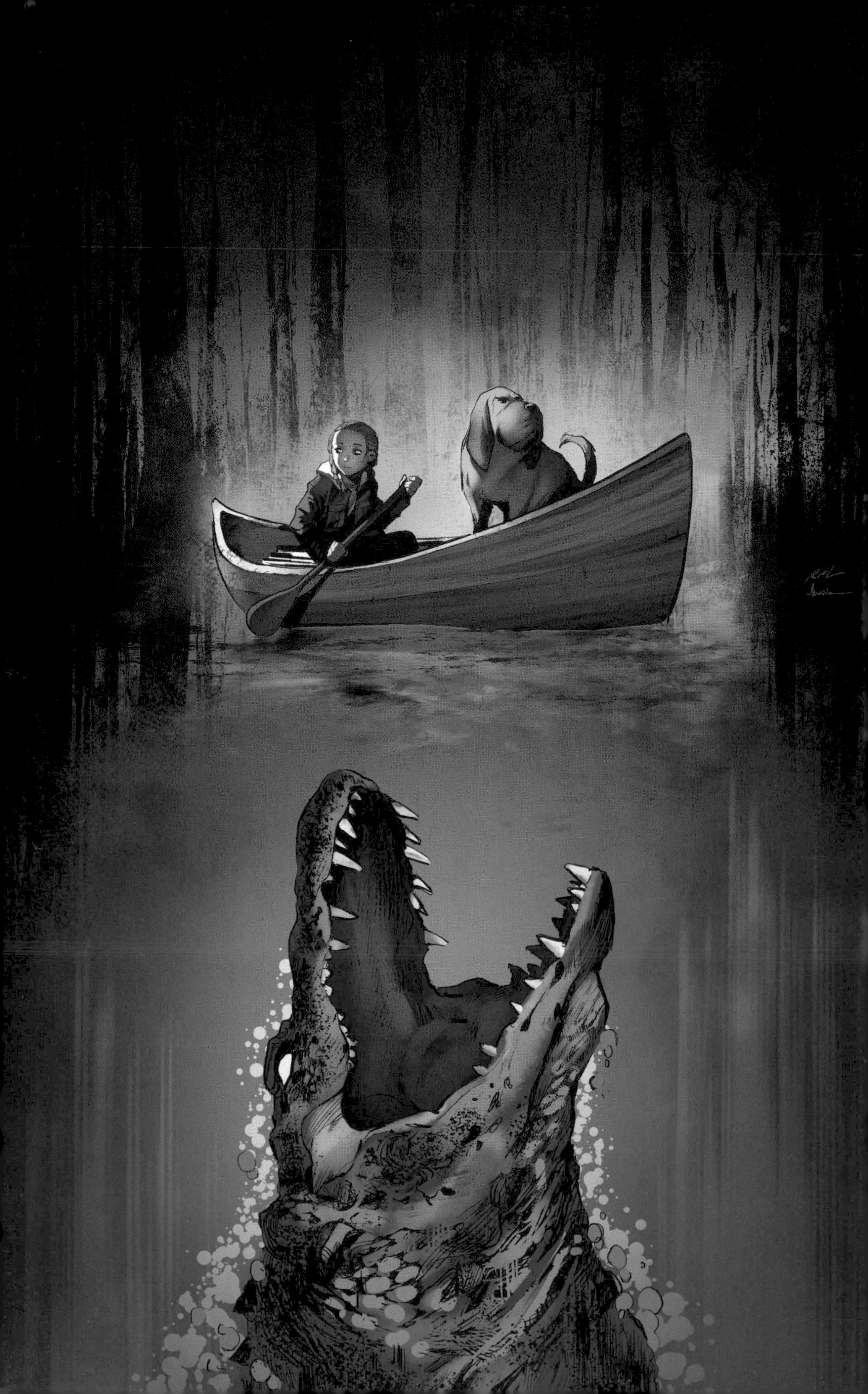

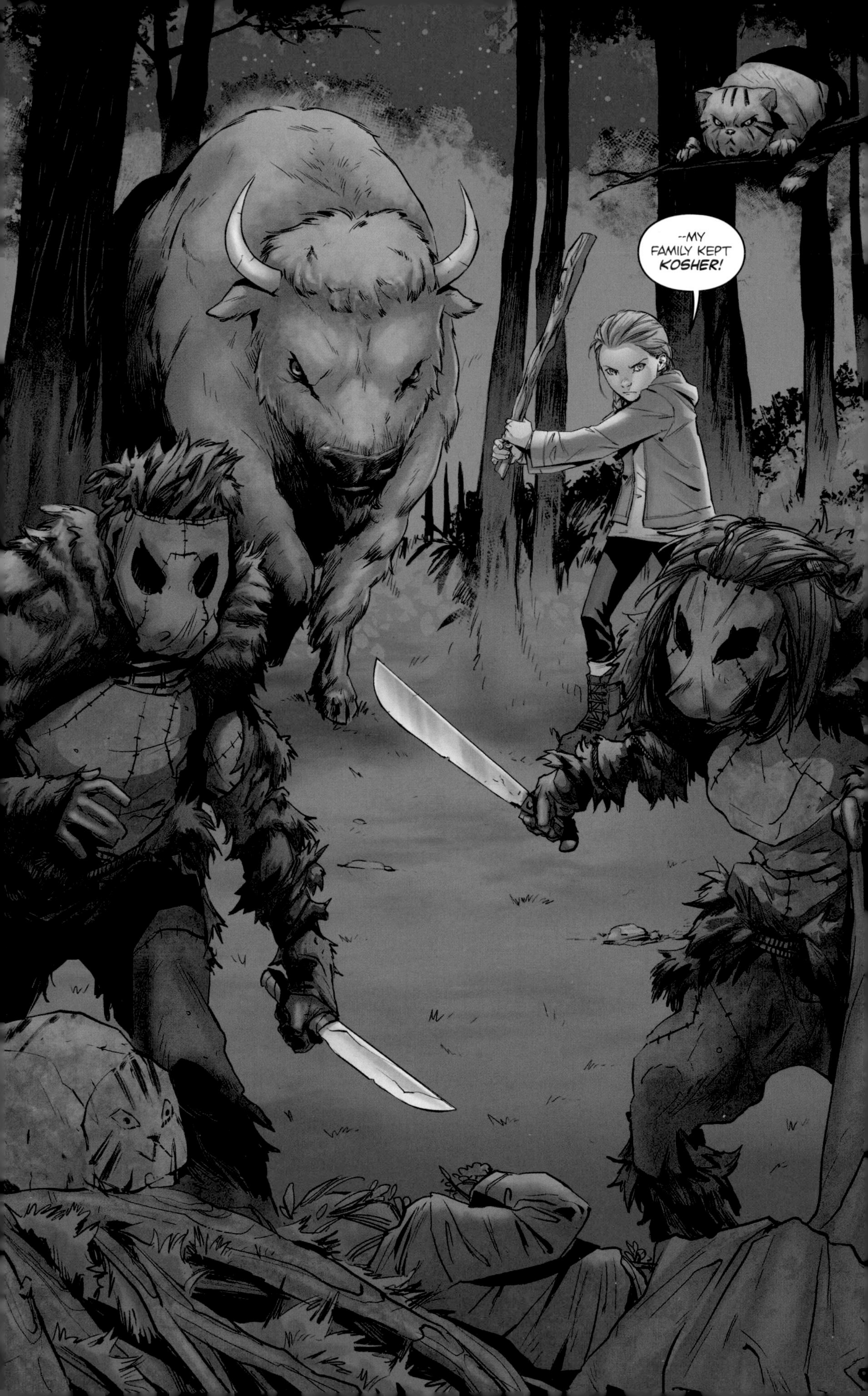
--MY FAMILY KEPT KOSHER!

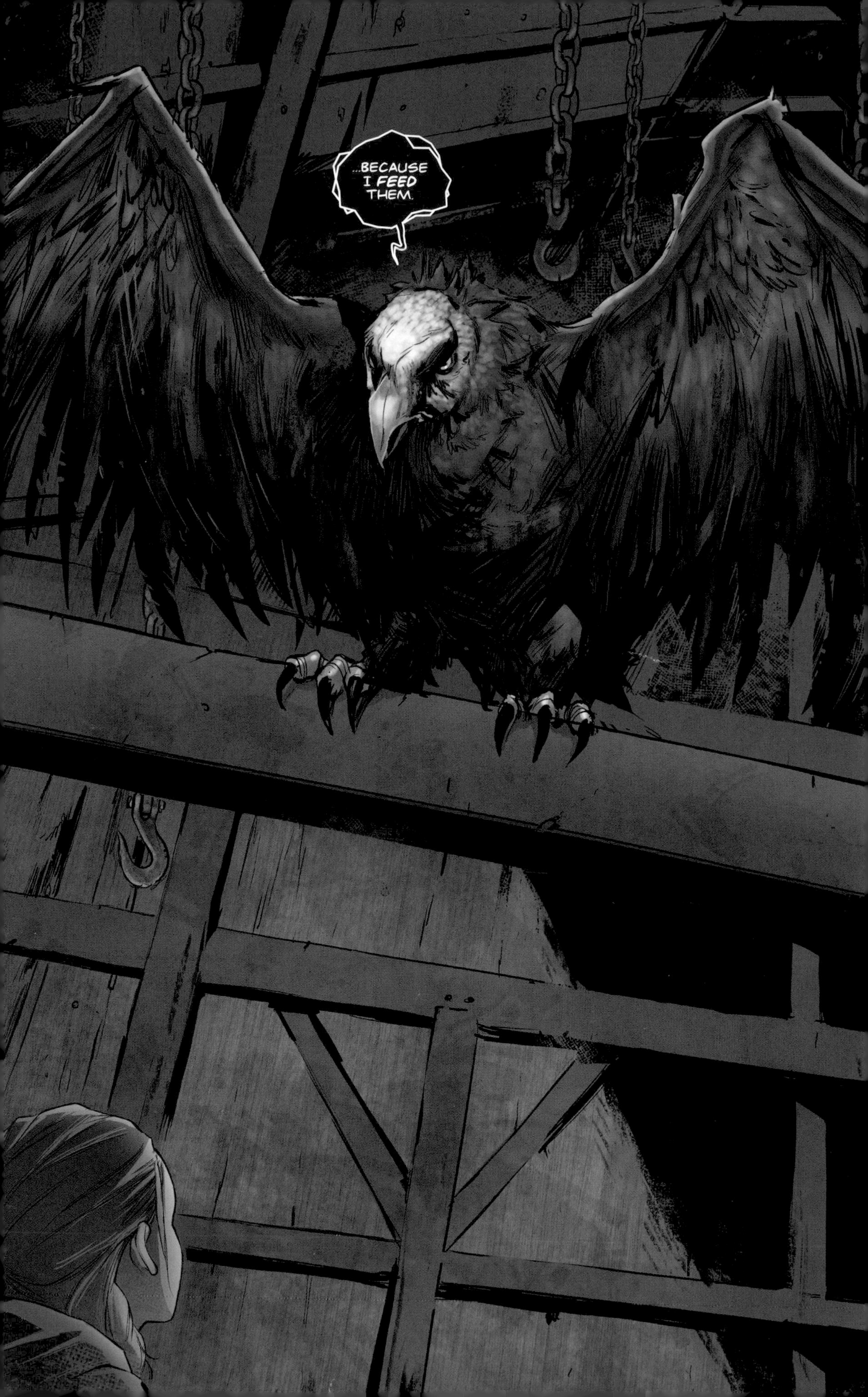
...BECAUSE I FEED THEM.

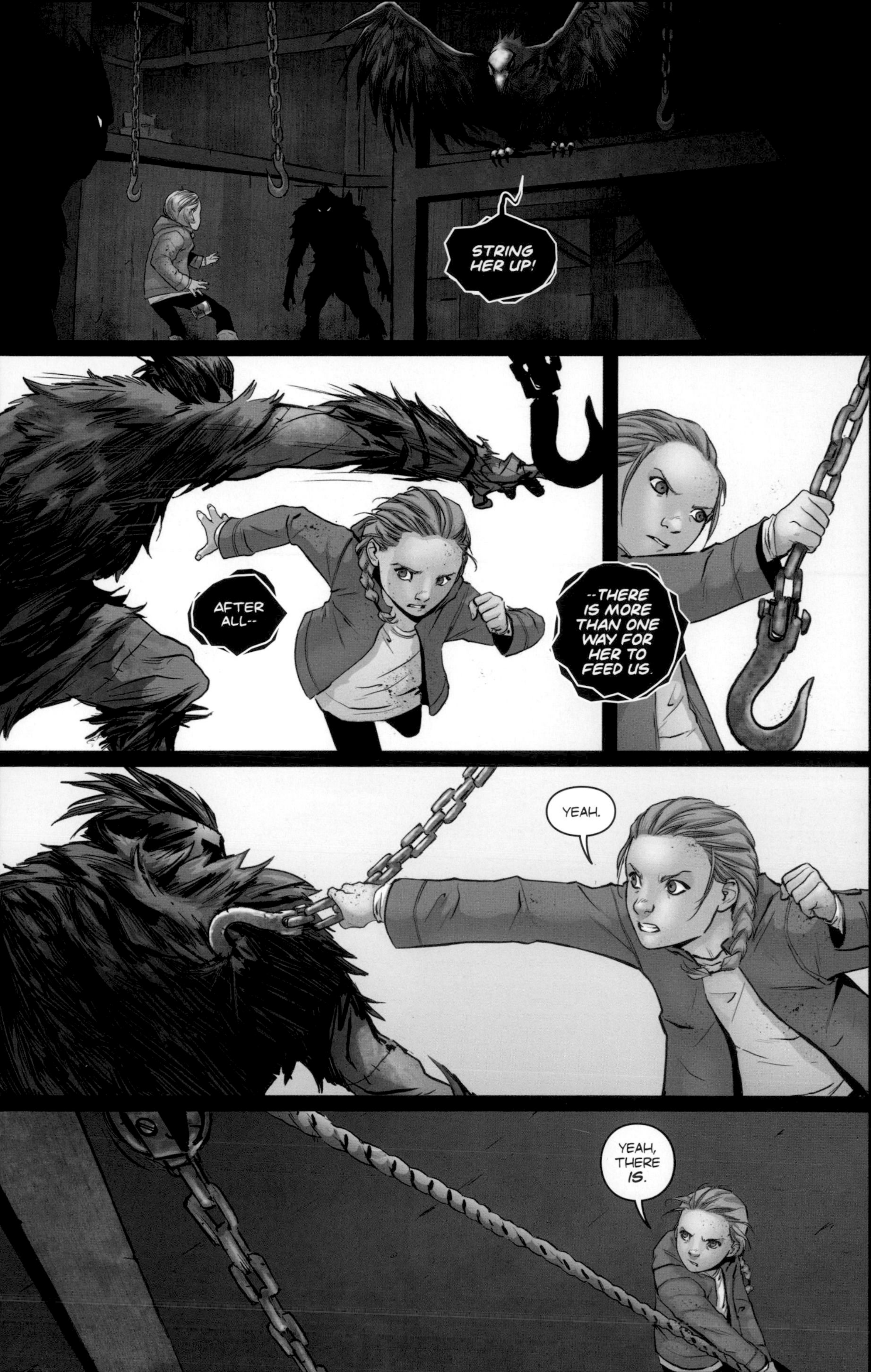
STRING HER UP!
AFTER ALL--
--THERE IS MORE THAN ONE WAY FOR HER TO FEED US.
YEAH.
YEAH, THERE IS.

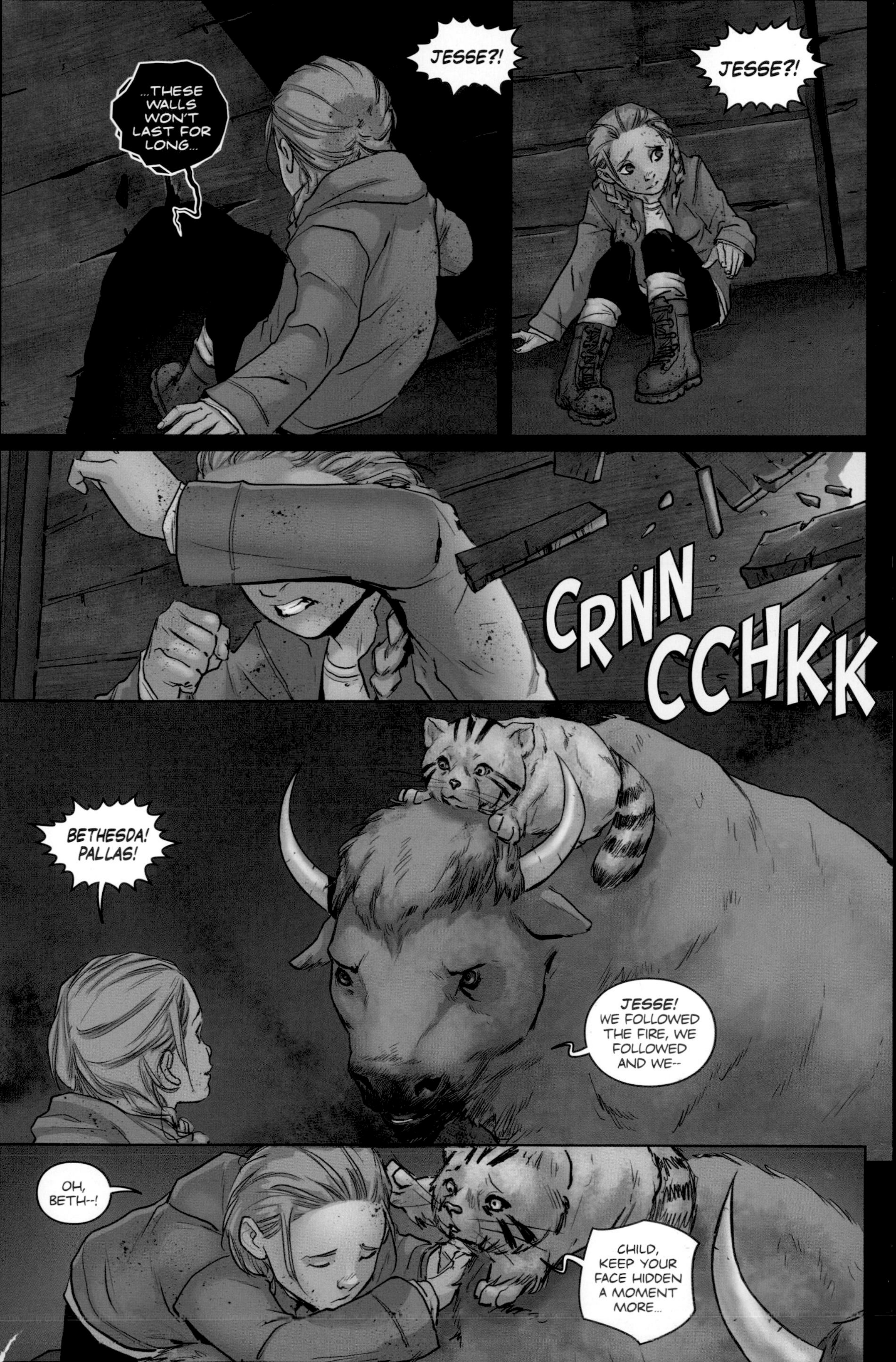
...THESE WALLS WON'T LAST FOR LONG...
JESSE?!
JESSE?!
CRNN CCHKK
BETHESDA! PALLAS!
JESSE! WE FOLLOWED THE FIRE, WE FOLLOWED AND WE--
OH, BETH--!
CHILD, KEEP YOUR FACE HIDDEN A MOMENT MORE...

TO BE CONTINUED...

# "FEEDING TIME"

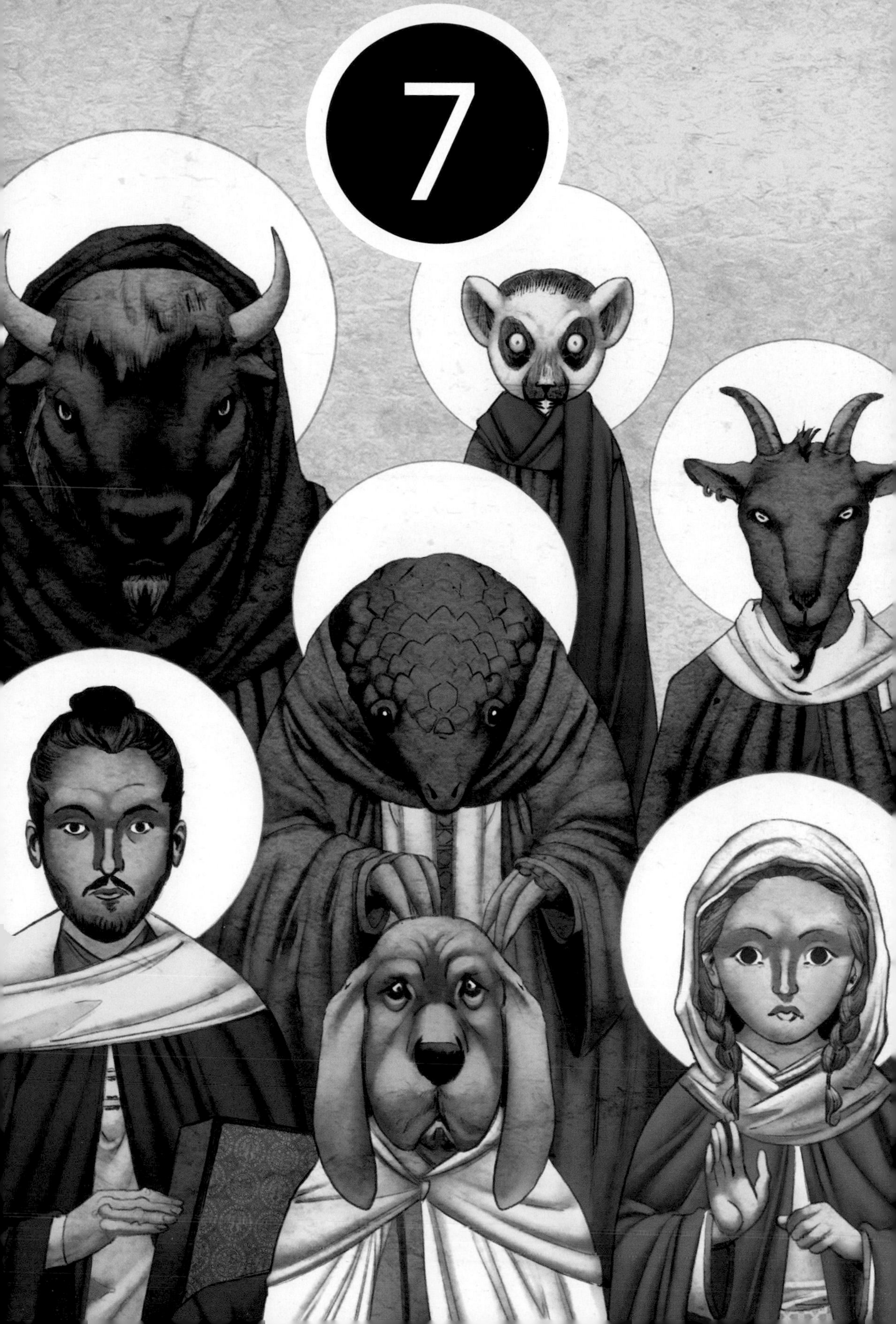
7

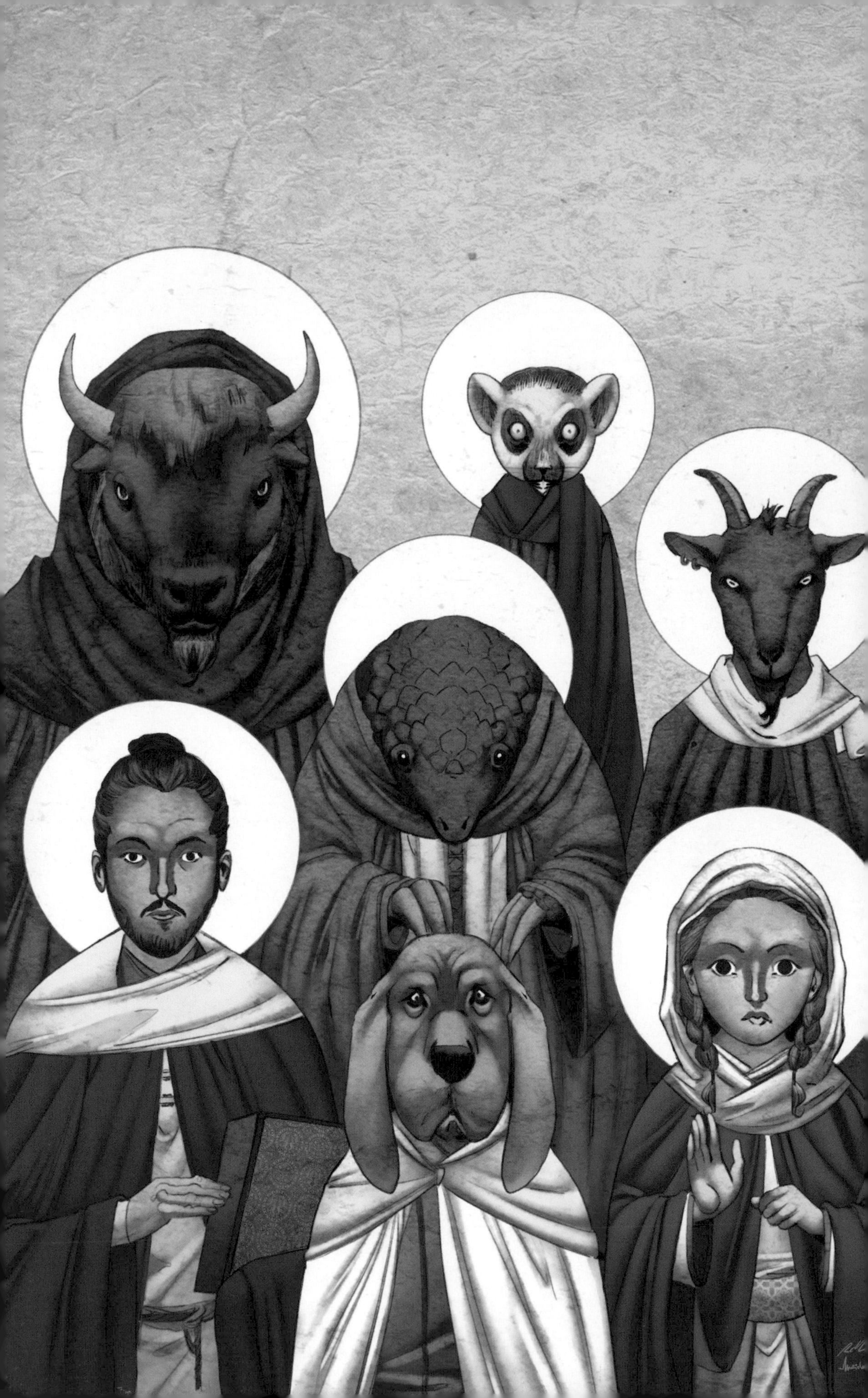

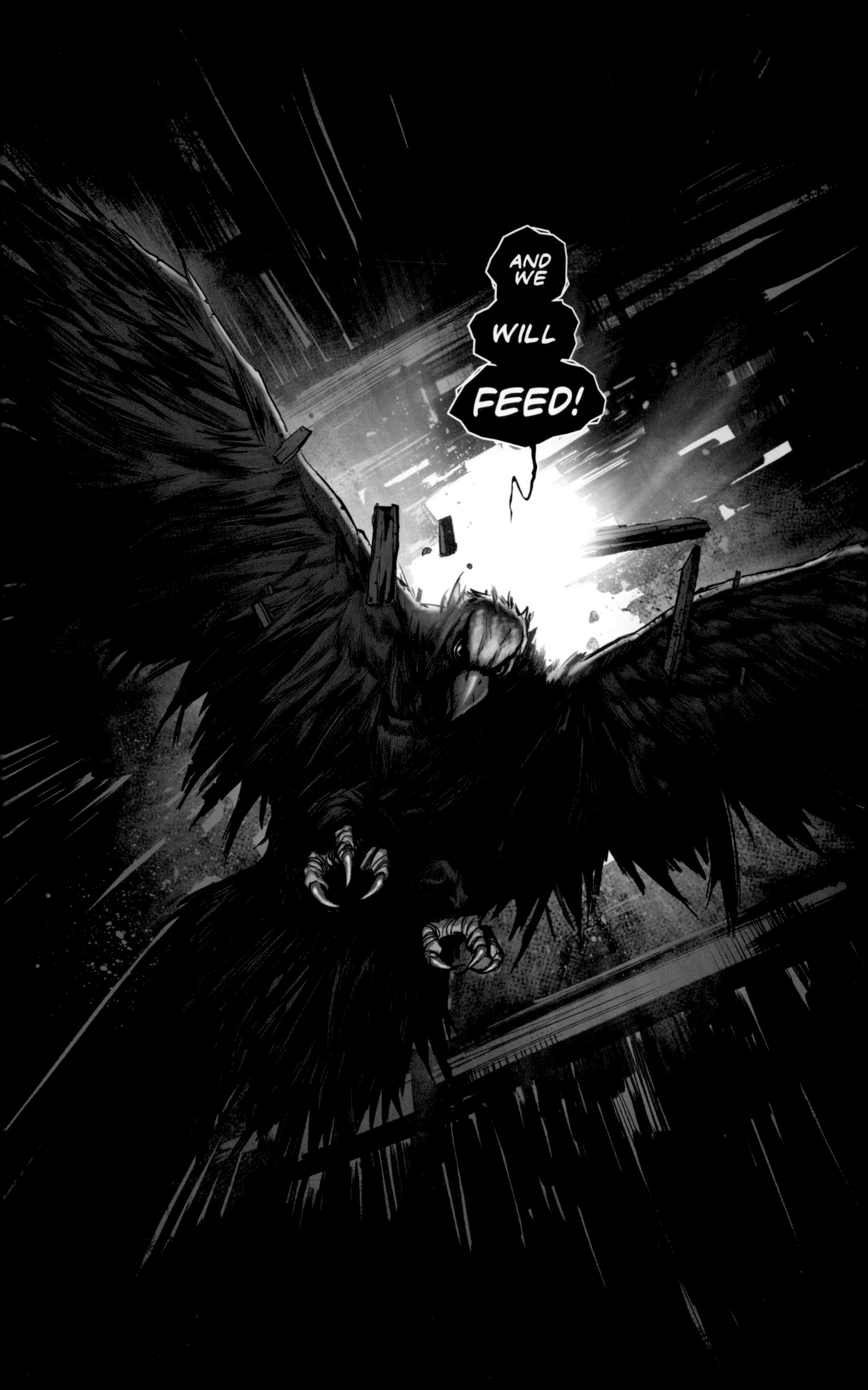
AND WE
WILL
FEED!

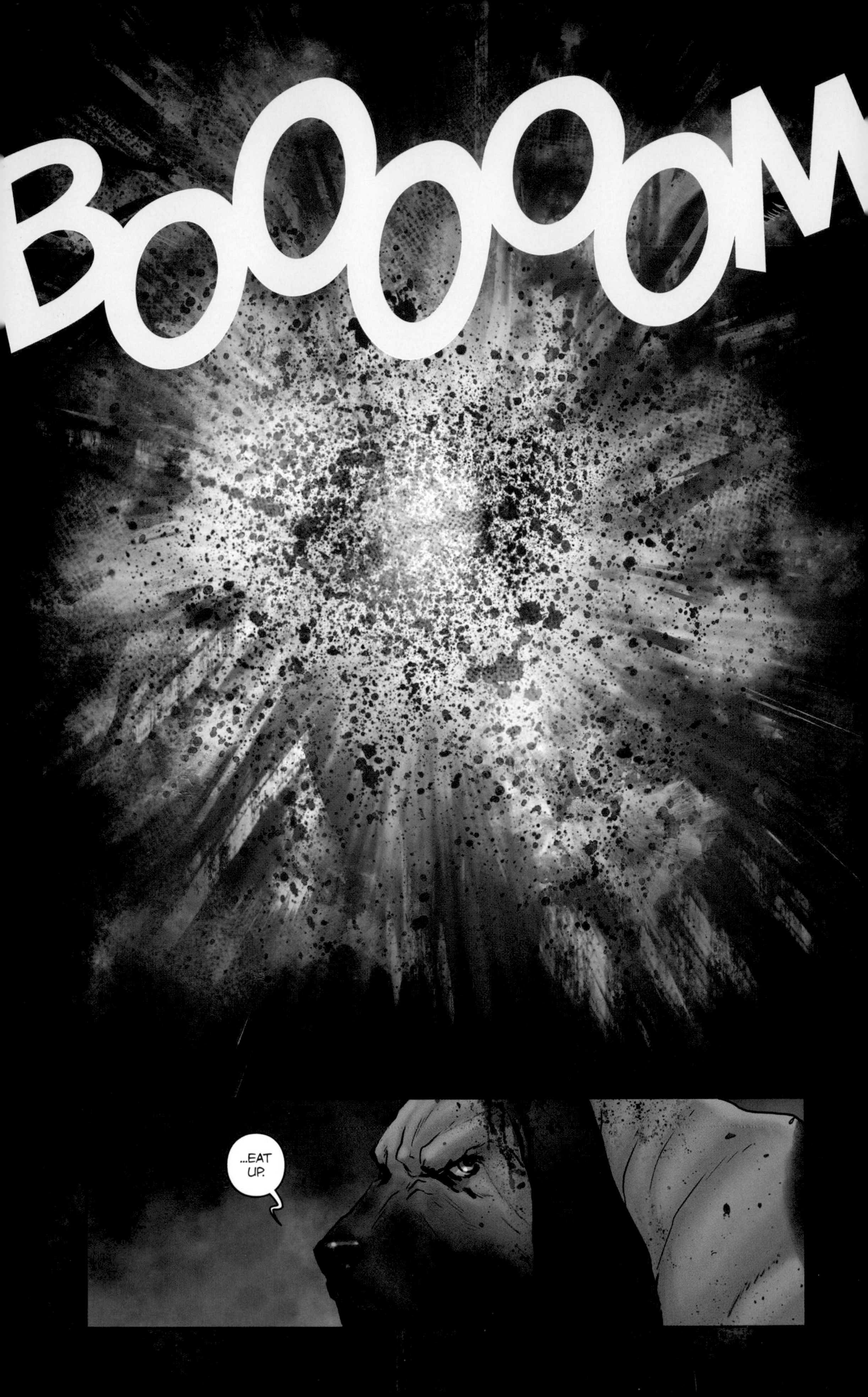
BOOOOOM
...EAT UP.

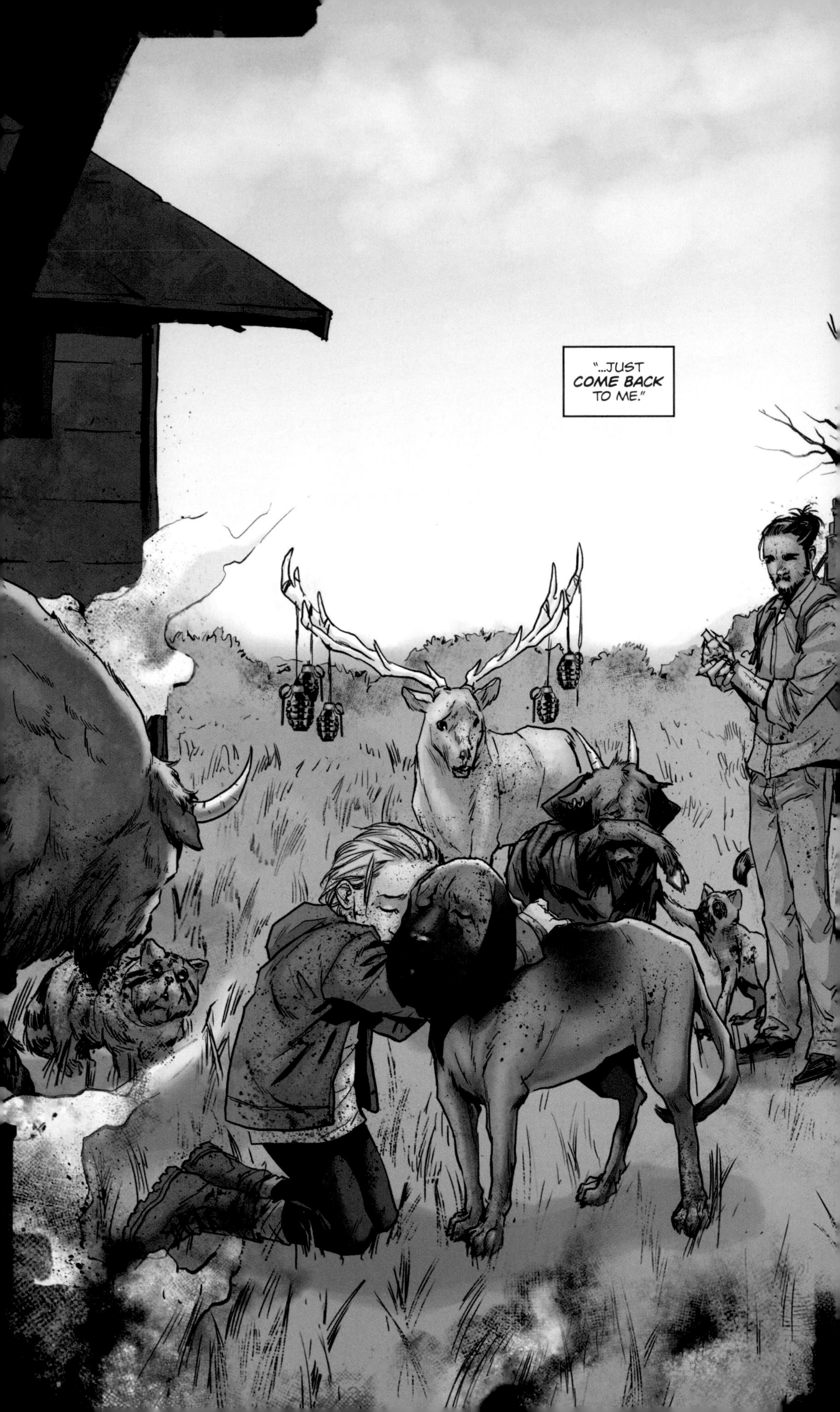
"...JUST COME BACK TO ME."

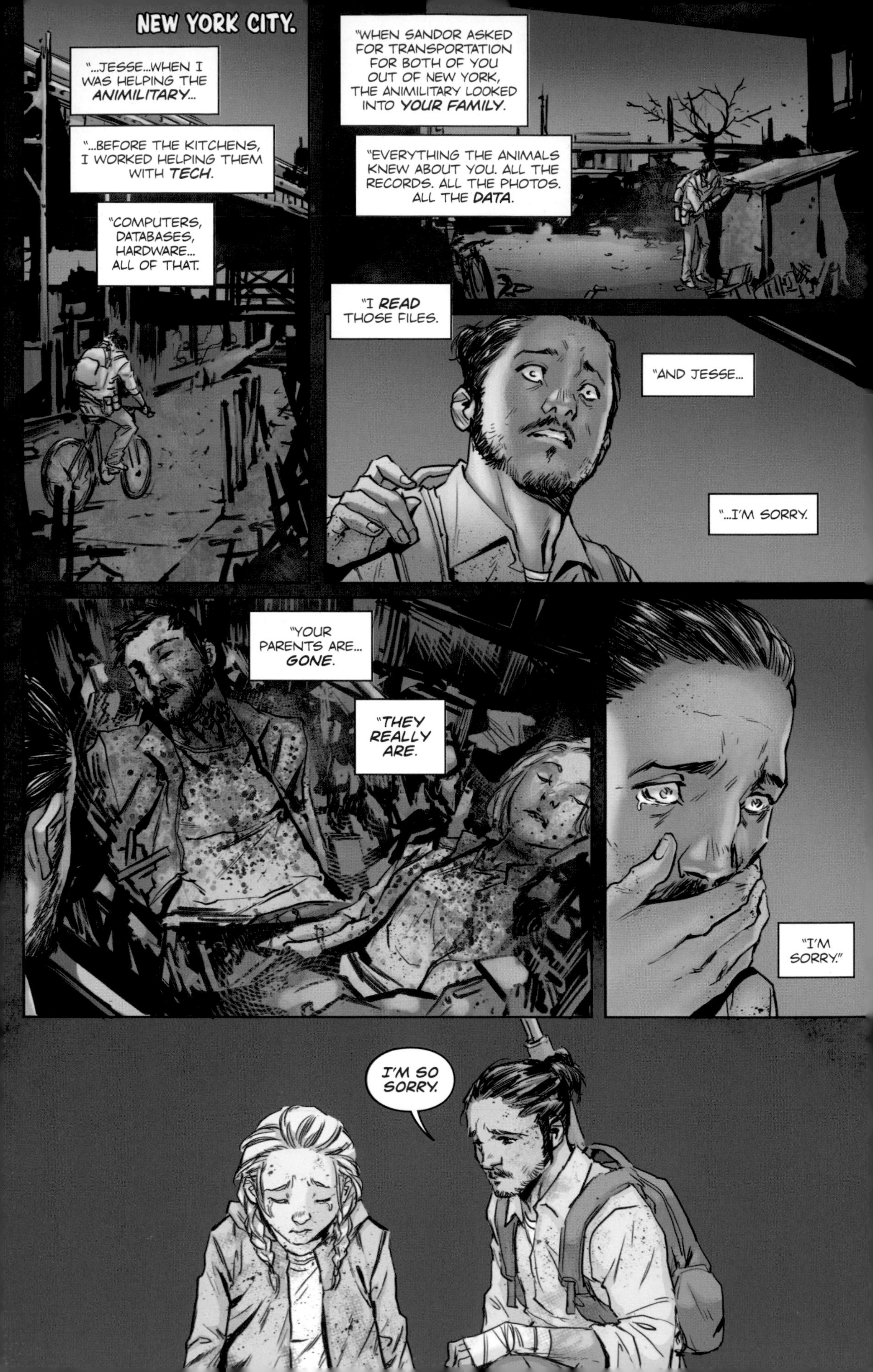
NEW YORK CITY.
"...JESSE...WHEN I WAS HELPING THE ANIMILITARY...
"...BEFORE THE KITCHENS, I WORKED HELPING THEM WITH TECH.
"COMPUTERS, DATABASES, HARDWARE... ALL OF THAT.
"WHEN SANDOR ASKED FOR TRANSPORTATION FOR BOTH OF YOU OUT OF NEW YORK, THE ANIMILITARY LOOKED INTO YOUR FAMILY.
"EVERYTHING THE ANIMALS KNEW ABOUT YOU. ALL THE RECORDS. ALL THE PHOTOS. ALL THE DATA.
"I READ THOSE FILES.
"AND JESSE...
"...I'M SORRY.
"YOUR PARENTS ARE... GONE.
"THEY REALLY ARE.
"I'M SORRY."
I'M SO SORRY.

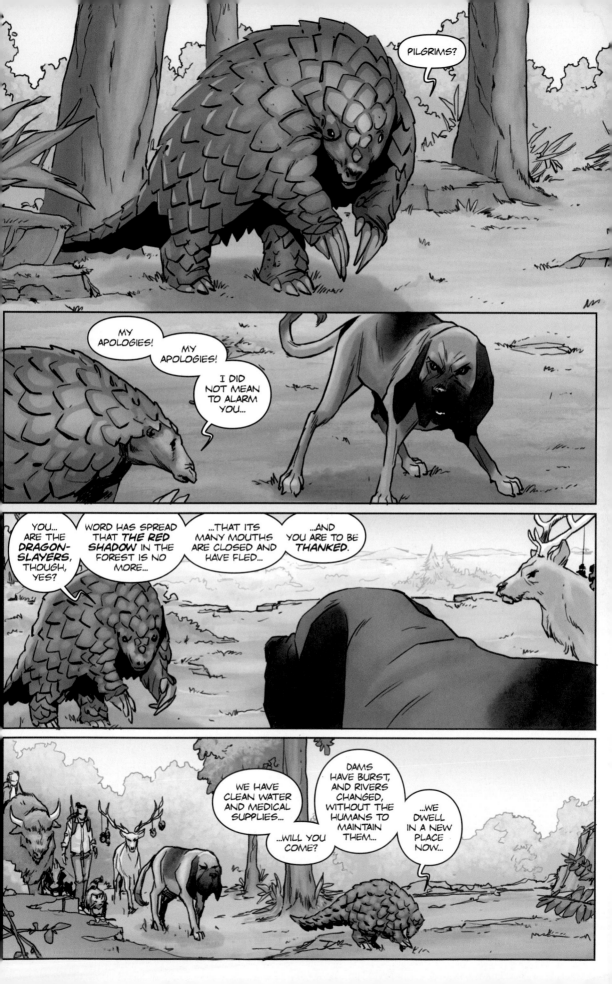

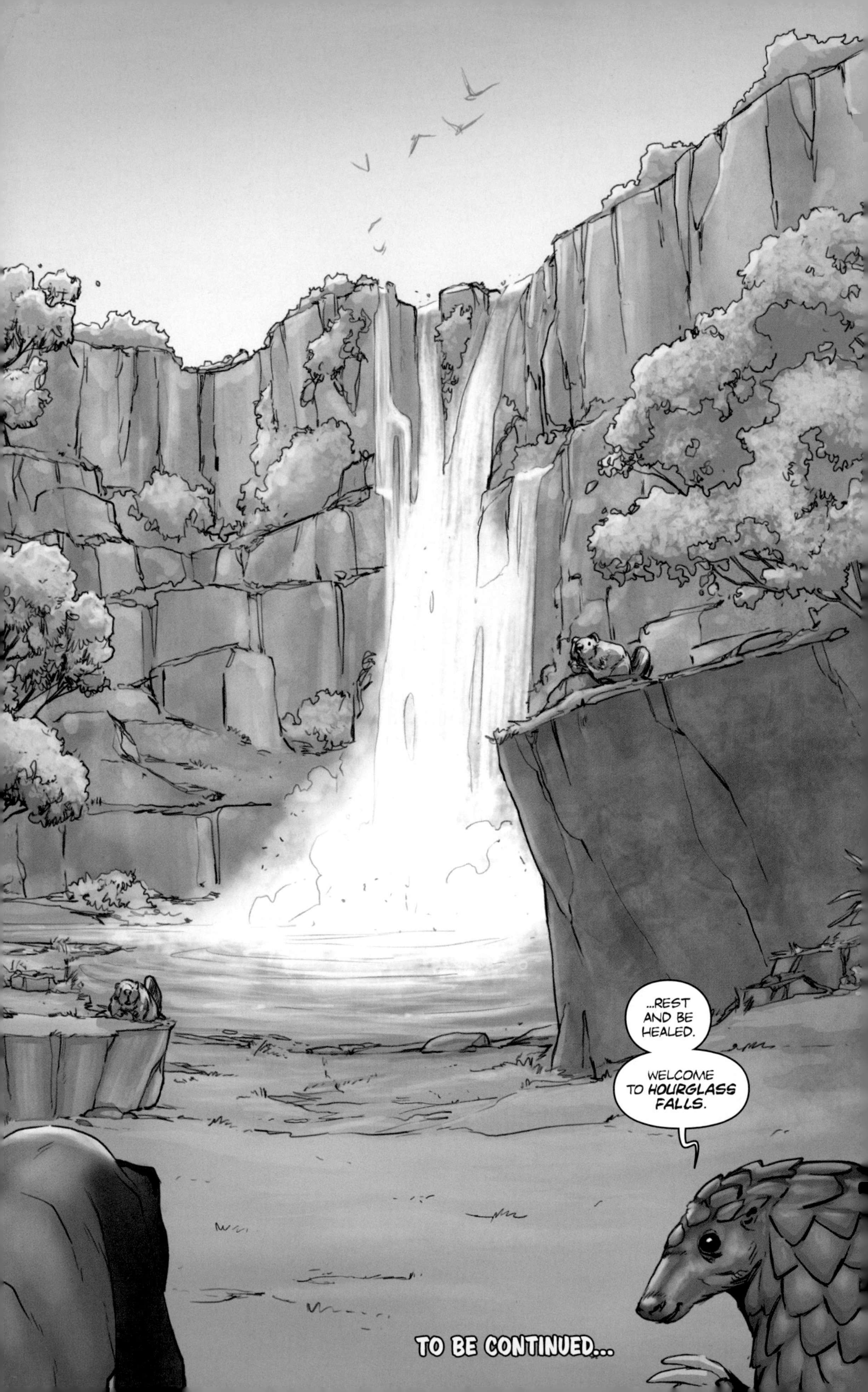
...REST AND BE HEALED.
WELCOME TO HOURGLASS FALLS.
TO BE CONTINUED...

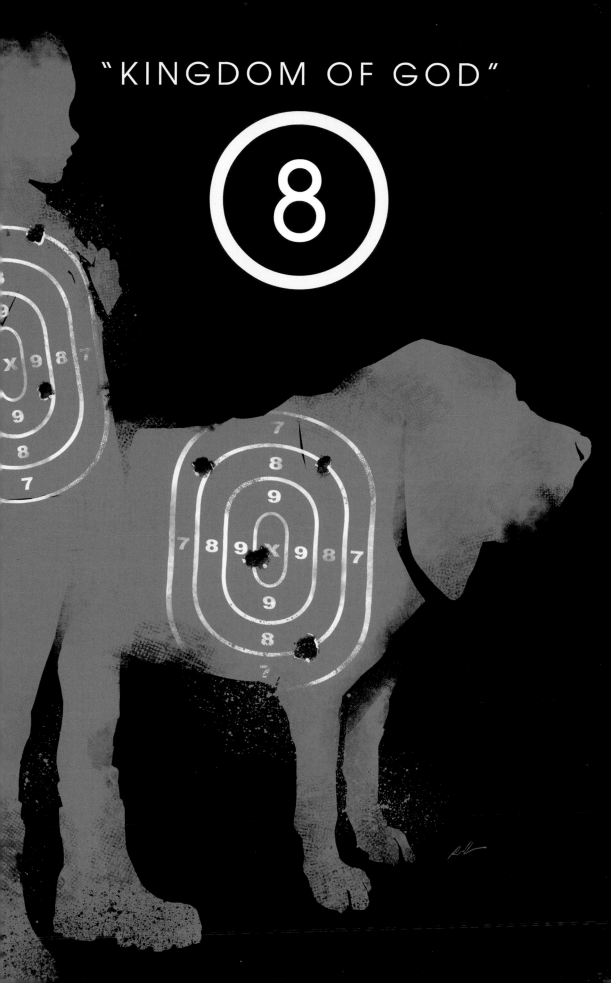

# "KINGDOM OF GOD"

# 8

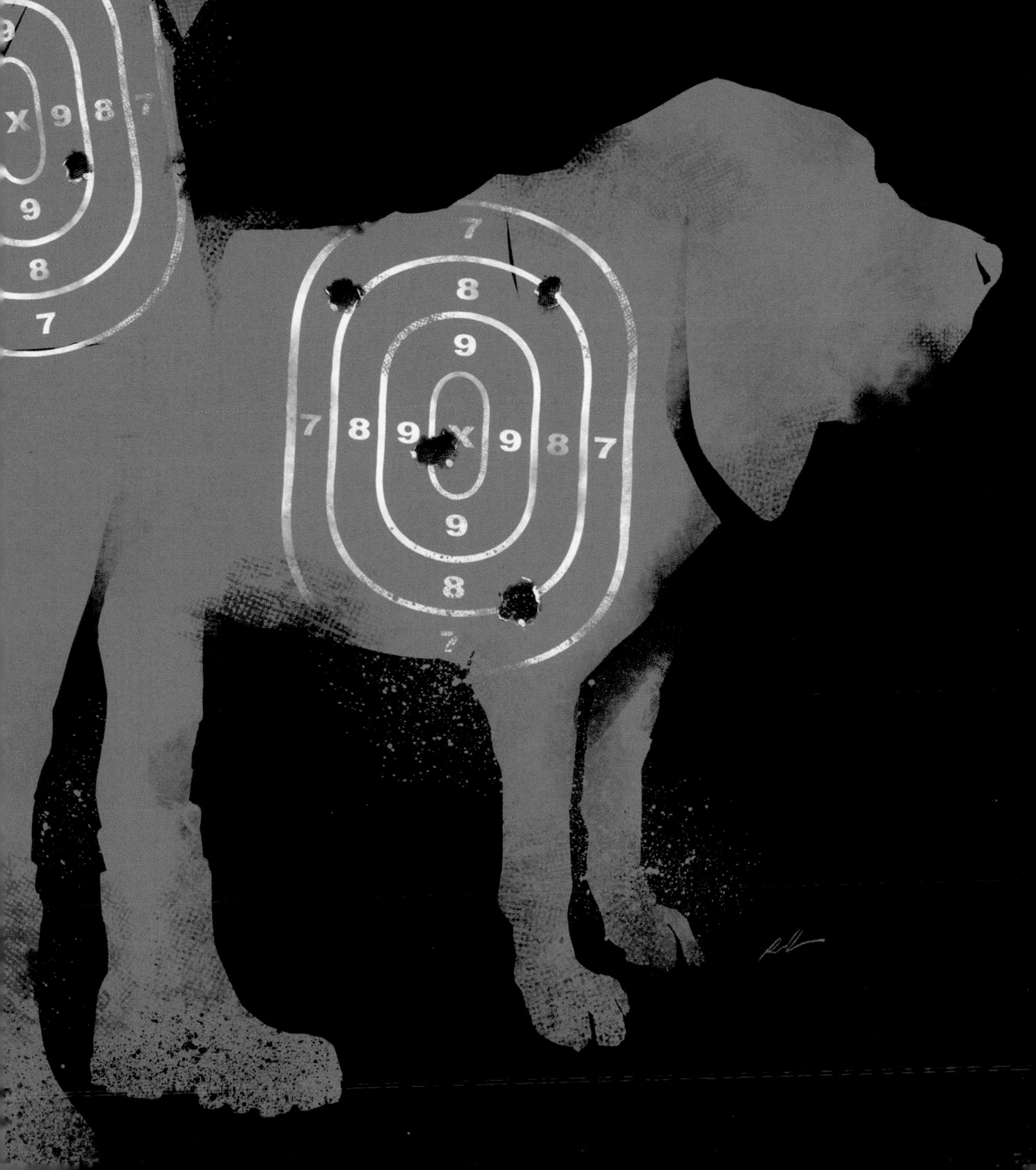

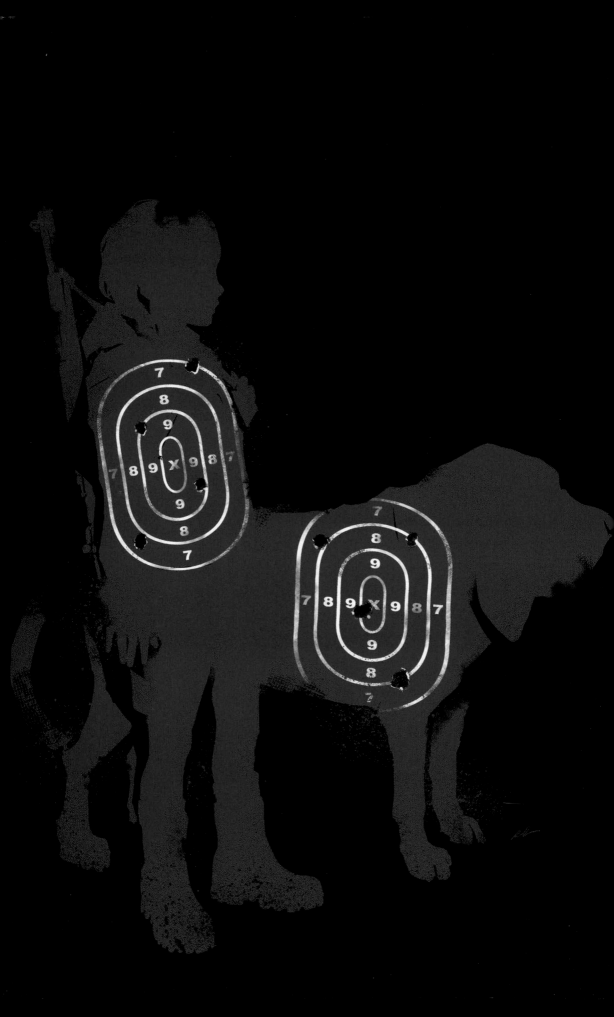

WE MET A MAN ALONG I-95 WHO SAID SOMETHING SIMILAR.

THEIR CAT-- A BODEGA CAT--WAS KILLED DEFENDING THEIR CHILDREN FROM LOOTERS.

HE TOLD US HIS CHILDREN HAD MANY QUESTIONS.

YES, I REMEMBER HIM.

THE QU'RAN DOES NOT ADDRESS THE MATTER, AND SO HE SPOKE TO AN IMAM WHO WAS HIS FRIEND.

"THE IMAM TOLD HIM THAT THE *ANGEL OF DEATH* TAKES THE SOULS OF HUMAN BEINGS, BUT OF THE SOULS OF ANIMALS, *NOTHING IS SAID.*

"THAT THEY HAVE SOULS IS NOT DENIED, THOUGH, AND IT IS PRESUMED THAT AS THE ANGEL OF DEATH COMES FOR HUMANS, *THE SOULS OF ANIMALS GO UNTO GOD,* AND THE ANGEL SIMPLY HAS NAUGHT TO DO WITH THEM.

"BUT THIS MAN WAS ONE MAN, WHO SPOKE ONLY TO THE UNDERSTAND-INGS OF ONE IMAM, AND DOES NOT PRESUME TO SPEAK FOR ALL, *LET ALONE FOR GOD.*

"ANOTHER WE KNEW TOLD US THE HOLY TEXT SAID NOTHING OF THIS, AND SO GOD DID NOT SEE FIT THAT IT WAS *FOR MAN TO KNOW--*

"--THAT WE ARE NOT TO TROUBLE OURSELVES WITH IT, BUT KNOW THAT WHEREVER THE SOULS OF BEASTS GO, IT IS FOR THE BEST, BECAUSE IT WAS DECIDED BY THE CREATOR.

"BUT THERE IS EXPECTATION THAT ALL OF US WILL BE GATHERED TO STAND IN JUDGMENT ON *RESURRECTION DAY,* THE HORNED AND HORNLESS, TO HEAR THE DIVINE JUDGMENT OF GOD."

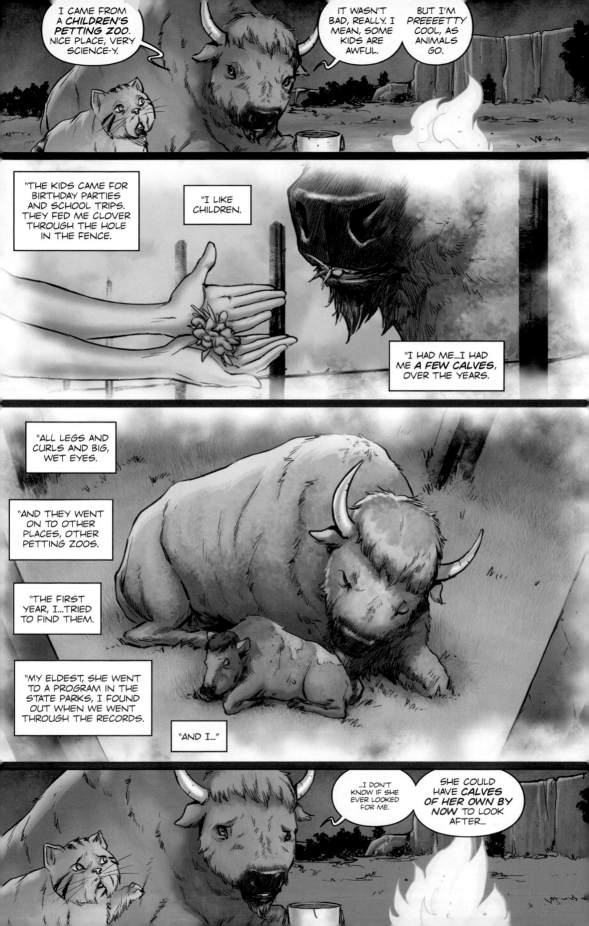

SOME SAY OF THE AFTERLIFE, IF A CREATOR LOVES US, AND MAKES OF HEAVEN ETERNAL HAPPINESS, **THEN ANIMALS SURELY SHALL BE THERE**, TOO.

"**THE LAST POPE** BEFORE THE WAKE DECLARED THAT ONE DAY, THE FAITHFUL WOULD SEE THEIR ANIMALS IN ETERNITY.

"**THE MORMONS**, BLESS THEM, HAVE ALWAYS PROCLAIMED THAT ANIMALS HAVE SOULS AND SHALL BE IN HEAVEN.

"**THE SIKHS,** TOO, SAY WE ARE ALL A PART OF GOD, AND THAT ALL SOULS ARE OF GOD, AND CANNOT BE DESTROYED--

"AND **HINDUISM** ASSERTS EVERYTHING IS A WHEEL, AND SOULS MAY ABIDE IN ANIMALS AND MEN ALIKE, TO DIE AND BE REBORN, EVERLASTING.

"--FOR IF WE CEASE TO BE ON EARTH, THEN WE RETURN TO HEAVEN, WHICH IS GOD, WHETHER BEAST OR BEING.

"AND IN **JUDAISM**, IF WE WEREN'T CONSIDERED TO HAVE SOULS BEFORE THE WAKE, WE MOST CERTAINLY DO NOW.

THERE'S AN ARGUMENT AND COUNTER ARGUMENT TO EVERYTHING.

"HOW MANY DEAD PETS CAN DANCE ON THE HEAD OF A PIN?"

AND WITH SO MUCH TO GET DONE, I AIN'T GONNA **TALK BIBLES** WITH YOU.

"AND THE **BUDDHISTS** SAY WE ALL HAVE SOULS--A SLIVER OF DIVINE BEING--BUT THAT WE RETURN TO THAT BEING ONLY TO BE BORN ANEW.

"TO THEM, THERE IS NO AFTERLIFE, AND NO REUNION, BUT DIVINE PEACE **FREE FROM PAIN**."

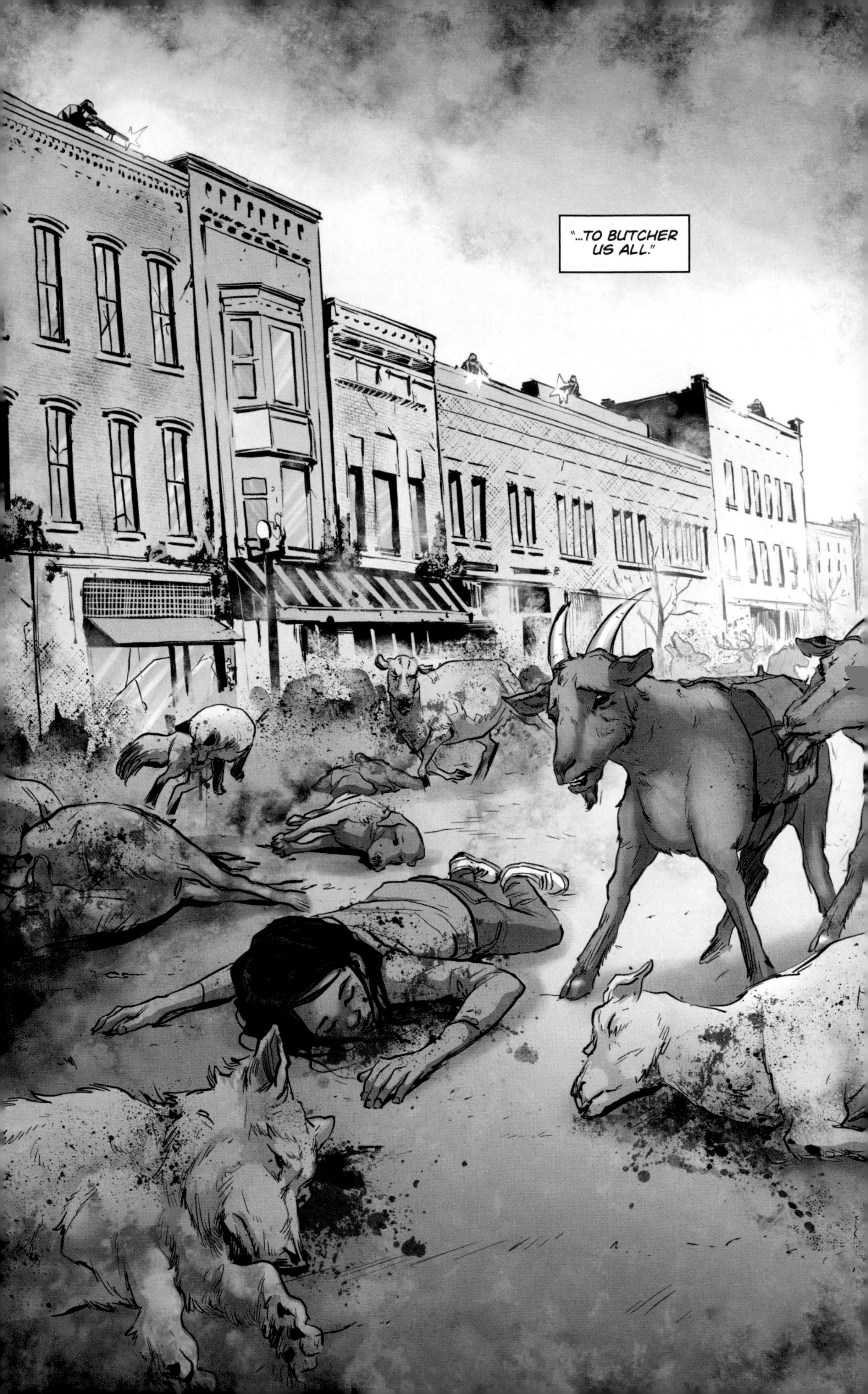
"...TO BUTCHER US ALL."

LONG PAST MIDNIGHT.

"THE WORLD OF ANIMOSITY"

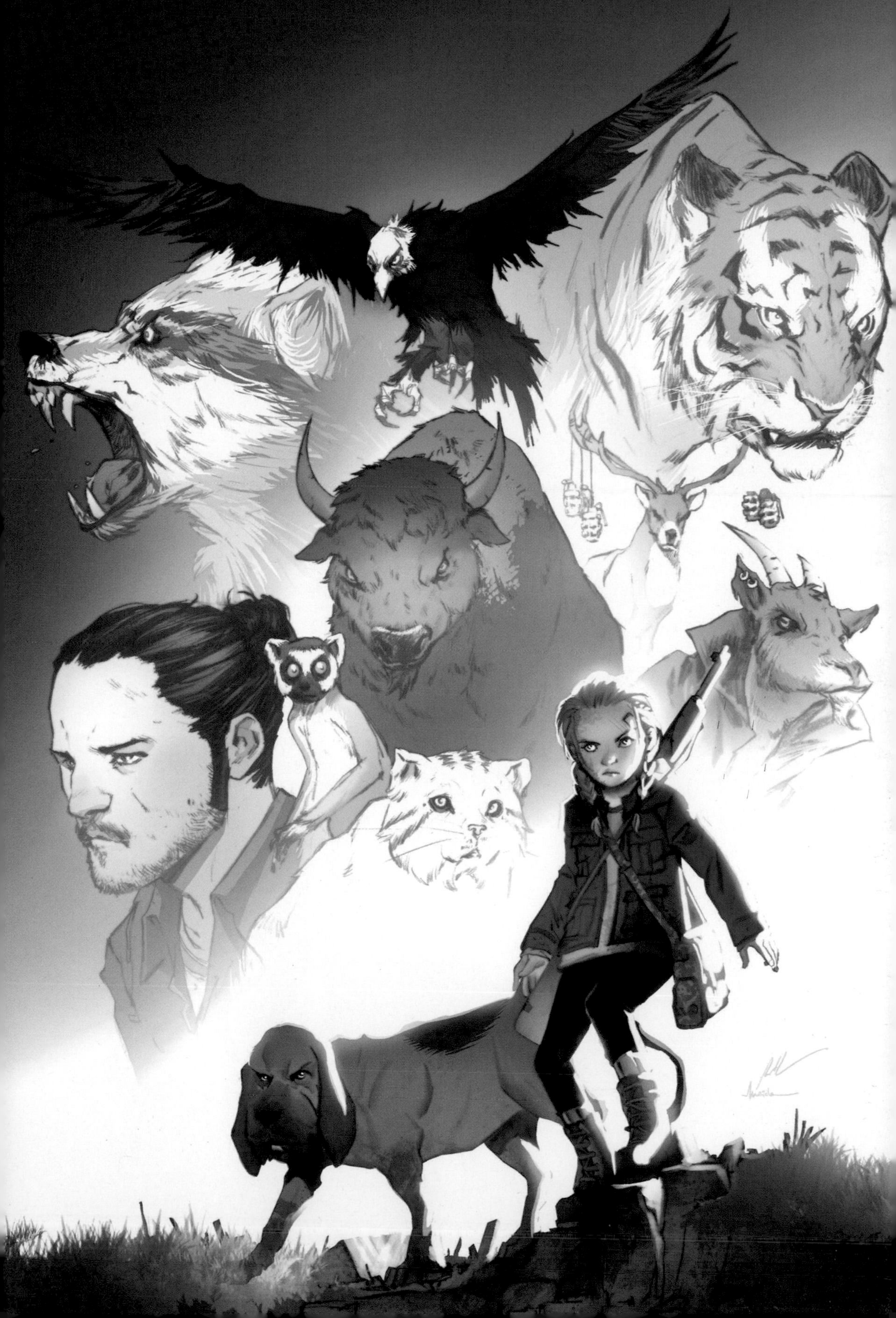

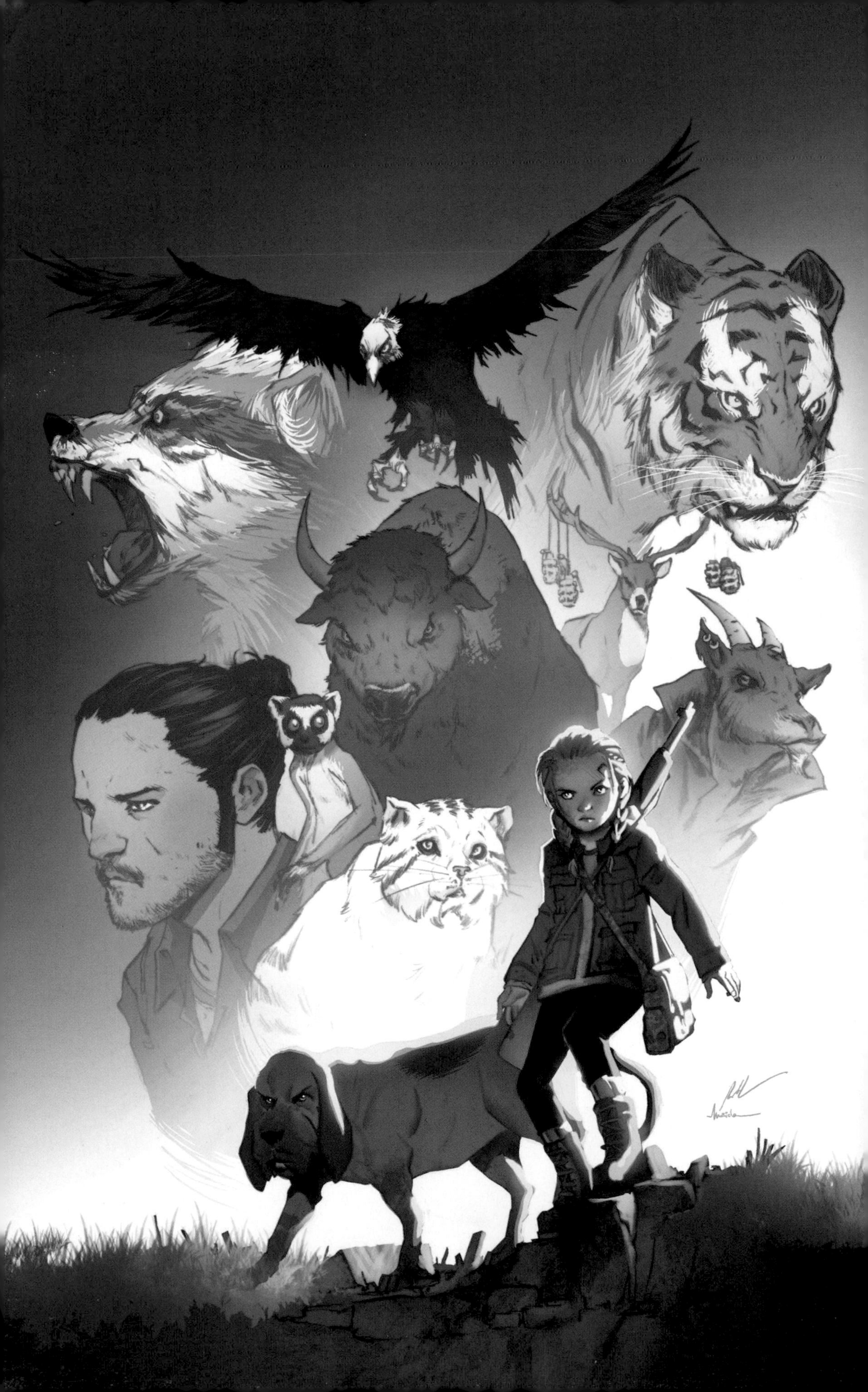

## THE PATH TO THE DOGHOUSE
### Animosity issues #1 - #8

On the day of the Wake, the Animals did just that—they woke up.

They started thinking. They started talking. They started taking revenge.

An orca at SeaWorld rose from his tank, all gnashing jaws and saltwater spray, to the screams of terror from the audience, only to slam down his flippers and declare undying love for his trainer—and a dog in New York City woke up to realize who and what he was, where and how he existed, and that the girl in front of him—his girl, his protector, his child, his Jesse—was more important to him than the sun and the sky and all the life that ever had been or will be. He belonged to her, forever.

But something happened in that city. No one's saying what.

And one year later, Jesse's parents are gone, and Sandor, her dog, her lone guardian, is getting her out—getting her far, far away, across the wild green yonder of America and all the way to the distant coast. There, in San Francisco, a city seized by the Animals, is Jesse's estranged half-brother, Adam.

Sandor did this because he has a secret.

Sandor is dying.

Purebred dogs of his ilk don't last long in the world, and he's had five good years—but now, he's got a ticking clock and a daughter he wants to see grow up happy and true.

Liaising with an agent of the Animilitary—an armed force of Animals seeking to create a separate and protected society—Sandor arranged for safe transport out of the princedom of New York City. In exchange, Sandor—a Bloodhound with a keen sense of smell—had to find one of the Animilitary's missing scouts. The trail uncovered a violent coup within the Animilitary, which had been facing a food crisis in the struggle to provide for all the Animals—carnivores, herbivores and omnivores alike—on a bloodless diet that could not sustain them. The coup exploded with Sandor and Jesse inside the camp, and they managed to make it out—along with certain Animals that Jesse had befriended—before the entire fortress was overrun by rebels and the vestiges of the American military.

Riding the back of the humpback whale who had originally ferried them across the Hudson River, Sandor, Jesse and their new companions moved down the coast until the path was clear and safe enough to begin a cross-country road trip.

Jesse is growing up, and signs of it frighten Sandor more than they even frighten her. Sandor fears, so much, that he will be unable to protect Jesse from all pain, all terror, aware that he will not be there for her adulthood.

But in the forests of Maryland came a dreaded specter—a creature like a great red dragon, vomiting fire and carrying off some of their companions. Sandor and some of the survivors go on the hunt, while two dear friends remain to guard Jesse—but the Red Dragon comes for them next.

The Red Dragon is revealed as a *lammergeier,* a red-bearded vulture with an eight-foot wingspan a belly of acid that dissolves bone. It rules its cult of men-masquerading-as-beasts and beasts-masquerading-as-men, compelling them to hunt in its name, and dividing the spoils among the squalid horde. The men-beasts of the woods listened closely to Jesse and her companions, marking their rivalries, their fears and their insecurities. They attempted to divide the band, snatching the smallest and weakest, separating them in the disorientating darkness of the woods. The beast-men sought to lure Jesse from her guardians, pretending to be her parents, calling to her as she slept—but Jesse awoke, discovered their true nature, and fought back.

Jesse, Sandor, and their companions destroyed the Red Dragon and its horde, with Sandor pleading for Jesse not to look, to protect her from seeing the true cost of her safety. Reunited, and mourning for their dead, the companions moved on through the hills—followed by a shadow shaped like the ghost of Jesse's mother—or the shape of the man-beast that had impersonated her.

The companions sought rest at Hourglass Falls, an isolated waterfall in the hills of Virginia, where creatures—human and Animal alike—come for a moment of peace on their way to greater journeys. The companions told their tales and origins, and speculated on the nature of their lives now—what they believe is left in life, and what they believe might be waiting for them in the great hereafter.

In this place, Jesse told Sandor that she knew of his secret. Sandor at last admitted the truth—his days are numbered, and he knows that he will eventually have to leave her. Jesse knows what death is now, and while she is unafraid, she will stay with him, and love him, because he is her dog—her good dog.

The specter of Jesse's mother's ghost—if that is what it was—dissolves into shadow and moonlight, and Jesse and Sandor fall sleep beneath the haze of stars.

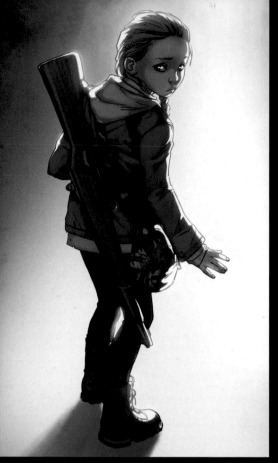

# JESSE HERNANDEZ

**Species:** Human *(Homo sapiens)*

**Age:** 11 years of expected 81 years

**Location Born:** New York City

**Mother:** Shannon Mandel

**Father:** Óscar Hernandez

**Siblings:** Adam North, maternal half-brother

**Height:** 4′6″

**Weight:** 72 lbs

**Hair Color:** Dark blonde

**Eye Color:** Amber

**Vorous:** Omnivore

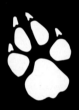

**Profile:**

Jesse [redacted]nandez just wants everybody to be happy, please[redacted] and safe, okay? And maybe nice to each ot[redacted]n if they don't always deserve it. She doesn't[redacted]hat happy means anymore, or safe, or [redacted]ot since she lost her parents, not since she lost [redacted]d she knew—but she's trying to remember, or, if she never knew, she's trying to find out.

Jesse was always shy and small for her age, and despite the best efforts of her parents, an early trauma rendered her lonely and anxious. Jesse never knew what it was she was supposed to be. If you're sweet, people say you're naïve, or boring, or manipulative, or stupid. If you're quiet, people say you're bitter, or judgmental, or needy, or doing it for attention. If she spoke in Hebrew with her mama, people called her one name, and if she spoke Spanish with her daddy, people called her a whole other one—and if you didn't know the name, you could tell in their voice wh[redacted] were trying to say.

Be[redacted]e Wake, people that Jesse didn't love always needed something from her, always expected somet[redacted]ing fro[redacted] her, whether it was teachers saying she c[redacted]n't try[redacted]hard enough with other students, or friend[redacted]arents trying to decide if she was "the right kind" [redacted]playmate for their daughter—whether it was old ladies telling her not to get dirty or men shouting things out of car windows that she didn't understand.

People were too much—too frantic, too frenetic, too busy, too demanding, too angry—Jesse wanted to just run up the stairs and into the elevator and up into her parents' New York apartment and slam the door and bury her face in a book and breathe in the warm, soft, blood-bay fur of her hound dog[redacted]dor. Sandor never asked her for anything, other [redacted]hat she stay with him. Sandor just let her be the [redacted]as, just be and grow and grow and be, and he [redacted] her a thousand fold.

After the devastating loss of her parents in the first year after the Wake, Jesse did not know what would become of her, and spent many days wishing she could go to sleep, in the same way that the Animals woke up—then she would never have to feel pain like this again. Only at Sandor's insistence, her goal is to reach her half-brother in San Francisco. Though Adam is a stranger to her, he is her only living kin, but she doesn't much care where she goes anymore—so long as Sandor, her Bloodhound, is with her.

Due to Sandor's stern methods, Jesse has been extraordinarily sheltered in the brave[redacted]ew world of the Animals. This allows her to gree[redacted]others with kindness and generosity, but also opens[redacted]her up to intense hazards and deceives her about t[redacted]ure of the dangers ahead. Jesse has long allowed[redacted]andor to think that his lies keep her in the dark—but about some

# SANDOR

**Species:** Bloodhound  *(Canis lupus familiaris)*

**Age:** 5 years of expected 7 years

**Location Born:** Freeport, Maine

**Mother:** Belladonna

**Father:** Unknown

**Siblings:** Six puppies

**Height:** 2'6"

**Weight:** 110 lbs

**Hair Color:** Red-brown

**Eye Color:** Hazel

**Vorous:** Omnivore

## Profile:

Sandor's entire mission in life is to give up the one thing that gives his own life any meaning.

Sandor was born to a Maine farmer whose prized hunting dog had a tryst with an unknown hound dog father who jumped the fence. Though he was the runt of the litter, Jesse picked him out when they were both little children. She guarded him, carried him, raised him, and on the day of the Wake, their roles switched—he became the caretaker, the protector, and she was his little girl.

Sandor was devoted to Shannon, Jesse's mother, but often clashed with Jesse's father, Óscar, over how best to protect and provide for the family. Far from the reluctant anti-hero, Sandor ardently strives to protect Jesse, but he is an ill-made knight—his intentions are powerful, but he is brutal, clumsy, earnest and vicious in defense of his child. He has done many things he isn't proud of, and a few things he *is* proud of that still won't see the light of day.

Sandor lies through his many sharp teeth to keep Jesse from understanding the ugliness of the world. He is frightened that one day his lies won't be good enough, and Jesse will see the world—and him—for what he believes both truly are.

As a large, deep-chested purebred dog, Sandor's life expectancy is winding down, and he is racing time

itself to carry Jessie through rivers, forests, mountains and plains to the one person he believes will take her in, the one person he believes could love her next to as much as he does—her half-brother Adam. Sandor's reasons for believing this are his own.

The whole momentum of Sandor's life is now in the flat-out race to bear his child to that safe haven—to see that she is happy, healthy, beloved and secure—and then, to lose her forever. Sandor's only happy ending is the thing he most fears—but isn't that true for all parents?

...Isn't it?

...Isn't it?

(Please, God, someone tell me what I'm doing is right.)

# THE FORMER UNITED

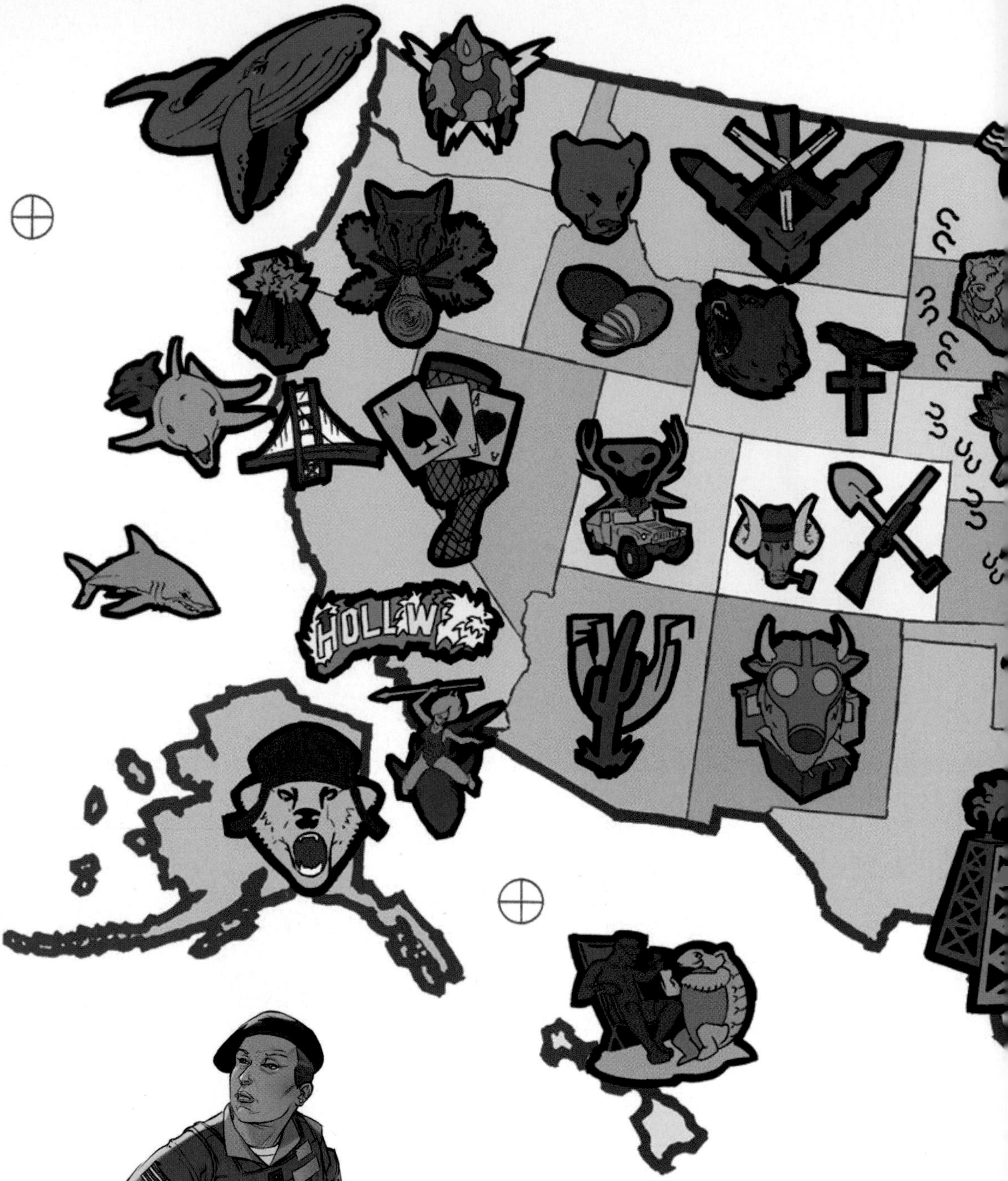

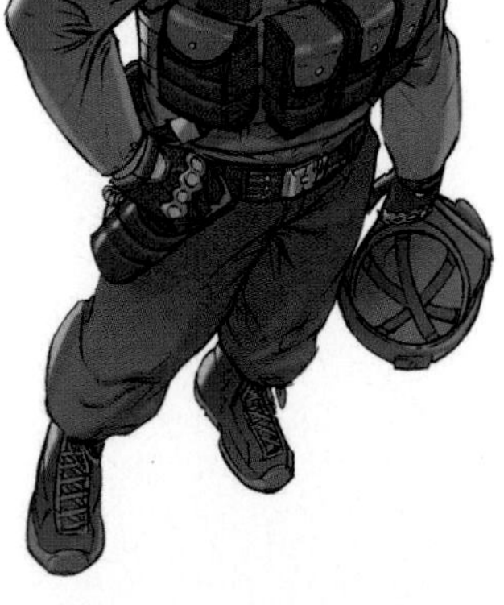

NYOTA GUTIÉRREZ

# STATES OF AMERICA

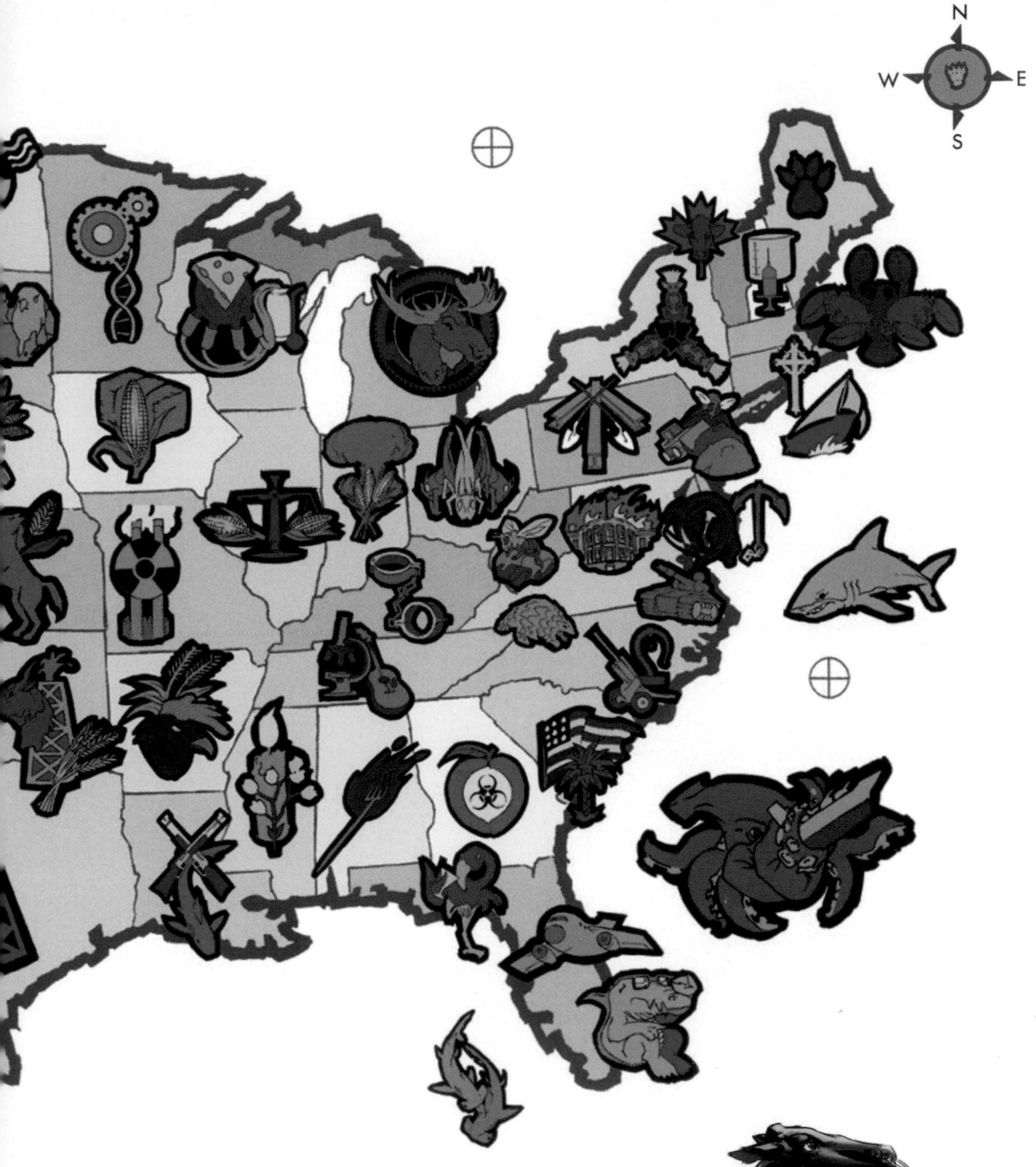
N
W
E
S

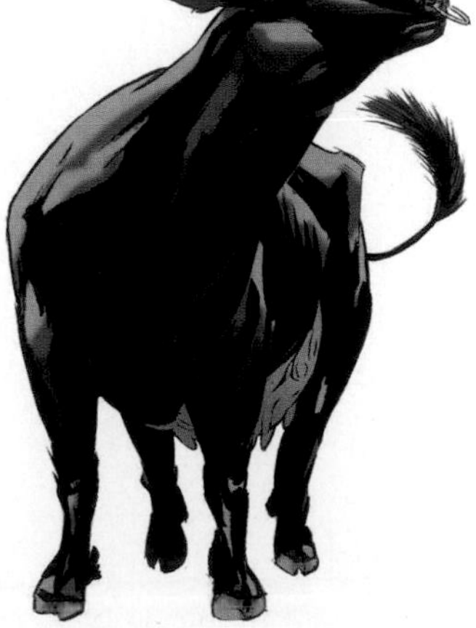

THE MAIDEN

## ALABAMA

In the initial crisis, the humans concerned themselves more with attacking each other in the chaos than defending one another against the Anima[redacted]sing. The conflict ended in a ferocious Animal victory after the Animals seized the Air Force and military bases and divided the vehicles, munitions and weaponry among themselves.

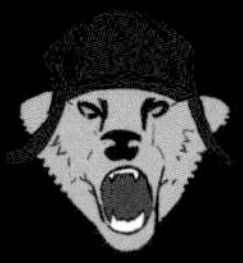

## ALASKA

Conditions unknown. Communications were seized and severed during and shortly after the Wake.

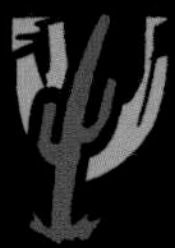

## ARIZONA

In the dissolution of any formal government authority on the continent, several Native reservations opened and expanded their borders, seized local power and negotiated truces among the Animal populations. These territories now operate as safe havens. Forces that have attempted to quell them have not been seen again.

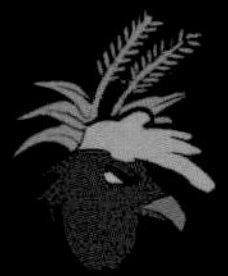

## ARKANSAS

Rich in rice and livestock, Animals seized many farms, and after initial acts of revenge, they maintain individual truces with human farming families. Individual farms allied themselves with Animal mercenaries to defend against invaders. Raids from other factions and other states are ongoing.

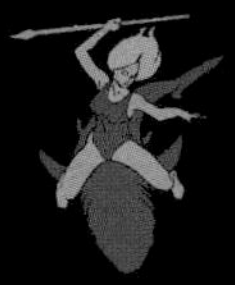

## CALIFORNIA

To the north, the redwoods and sequoia forests have become notoriously haunted by spectral creatures of species unknown. In San Francisco, the Animals seized power with the smallest loss of life seen in a city of this size, and currently struggle to rebuild a functioning society where humans and Animals might live together. To the south, looting and debauchery are rampant as many humans and Animals welcome the end of the world and live out their numbered days in hedonism.

## COLORADO

The only known location in the United States where an Animal force—led by [redacted] a bighorn sheep—has seized a nuc[redacted]o. The society is isolated and well defended, and little additional information has been attained. Military fighters sent to bomb the area were taken down by individual birds who sacrificed themselves by diving into the engines of the planes or flying into the paths of oncoming missiles before the payload neared the city.

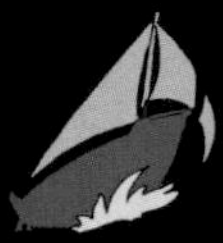

## CONNECTICUT

On the day of the Wake, wealthy humans attempted to hole up in suburban homes, but Animals, anxious and eager for comfort, entered these luxurious neighborhoods house by house, seeking beds, pillows, air conditioning and bathtubs. The human population tried to flee by boat, presuming that the Wake had not extended to the ocean, and many were sunk on private sailboats and yachts by the less-than-sympathetic creatures of the sea, despite the attempts of many Animals to rescue them. The surviving humans are currently held for ransom against whoever will redeem them.

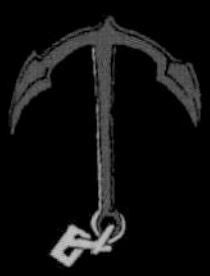

## DELAWARE

Humans retreated to the massive shipping yards, which became bunkers against Animal invasion. The Animals soon lost interest in pursuing the humans, and some humans tentatively reemerged. Other human colonies still sit in the harbors, self-contained within the ships and their various cargos, utterly isolated against the outside world, and forming mad, miniscule new societies within these strange, floating cells.

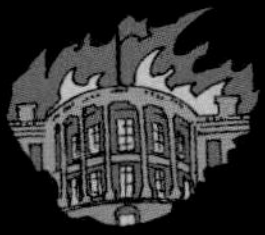

## DISTRICT OF COLUMBIA

Bo, Socks, Barney and Buddy could be trusted. This pet couldn't be.

## FLORIDA

Dinosaurs vs. Florida Man, live on Pay-Per-View. The happiest place on earth to enjoy the end of days.

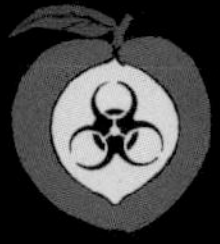

## GEORGIA

The Center for Disease Control in Atlanta—which houses the United States' cache of ferociously deadly diseases—is besieged by Animals. Scientists within struggle to find a way to defend humankind with bioweaponry, while Animals seek to prevent the use of these viruses against them. Both human and Animal radicals seek to control fatal strains of plague that could be released upon the world.

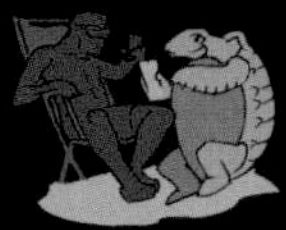

## HAWAII

"We live in peace, mostly. Agreed just to kill and eat the fish and live as pescetarians."

"Don't the fish scream?"

"Of course they scream! You just...you just try not to hear it, after a while."

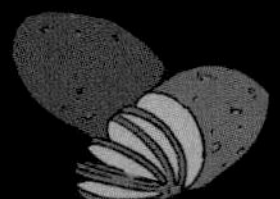

## IDAHO

Idaho faired quite well among the fates of the United States. The high agricultural production from potatoes and the low human population permitted the humans and Animals to reach a tense, if tidy, trade agreement to mutually harvest the crop. While monotonous, and undoubtedly contributing to a kind of madness through boredom, Idaho was never plagued by starvation and is largely secure post-Wake.

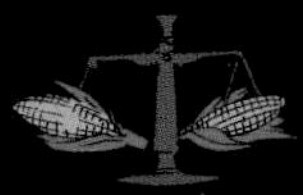

## ILLINOIS

In Illinois, the bedraggled vestiges of human lawmakers desperately attempted to assess the legality of this bizarre new world. What rights do Animals have? What rights do humans? Where does property enter into all of this? What is now considered murder? Can you be tried retroactively for violence committed before the Wake? Who owns what? What happens now? Oh God, oh God–

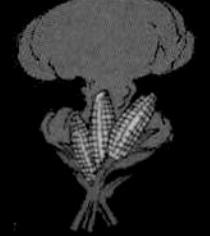

## INDIANA

Human separatists poisoned huge fields of corn, killing hordes of Animals and securing their own store of food from the bodies of the dead. However, the poison—a rare fungus—mutated, and massive areas were bombed to prevent the spores from spreading.

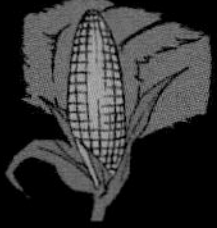

## IOWA

Much of Iowa was divided and annexed for food production. Various powers rode in to conquer and kill those in power, but those laboring in the fields—whether enslaved or free—largely stayed the same. One of the only states not to suffer starvation, but one of the only ones to suffer spontaneous civil wars every few weeks.

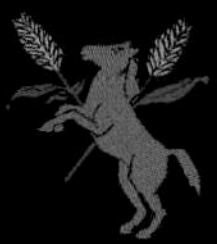

## KANSAS

The heart of the kingdom of the Horse Lords, radicals advocate for a separate Animal nation of herbivores in the breadbasket of the former United States. They are led by the triumvirate of the mare Angharrad, the gelding Incitatus, and the stallion No Name, and offer citizenship only in exchange for labor and abiding by their strict, Draconian laws.

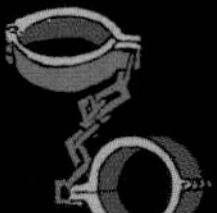

## KENTUCKY

The humans in rural Kentucky currently hold their own, maintaining as close to a pre-Wake society as possible, paying or forcing the Animals to abide in their original roles. The mountains are currently targeted by Animal rebels who are planning a siege of the hills.

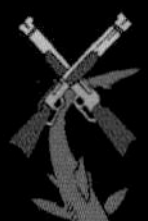

## LOUISIANA

In Louisiana, the sprawling prison system orchestrated a mass release of inmates who were offered full pardons in exchange for fighting the Animal uprising. Many fought for the humans, and many defected to the side of the Animals in exchange for the security of their families. The conflict is brutal and ongoing.

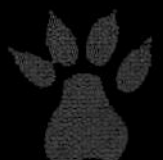

## MAINE

Despite extraordinary resourcefulness by the humans, the state fell to the Animals, who were able to use the dense foliage, fog and forest to their advantage. The state has been sealed, and is rumored to be controlled by a creature who rises at night from the crossroads.

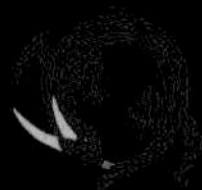

## MARYLAND

The forest of Maryland is home to the legend of a bloody red dragon who sprays fire and acid from its throat and devours creatures whole. The dragon is said to be served by a slave-army of shambling man-beasts and beast-men who worship it in exchange for food and protection. To enter these forests is certain death, for these creatures keep the old ways of blood and bone and, above all, hunger.

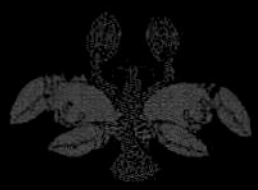

## MASSACHUSETTS

The dense urban area created a bottleneck for humans seeking to flee, and the coasts became the major source of danger as crabs, lobsters and other crustaceans surged onto the beaches and up from the sewers, while sharks, dolphins and some whales entered the cities through rivers and reservoirs. Two-thirds of the cities have been conceded to the Animals, who have gone about remaking them to their own tastes, dressed in seaweed, the streets flooded and drains overflowing. Conflict is ongoing as humans fight back, including a secret rebel militia wielding Red Sox bats.

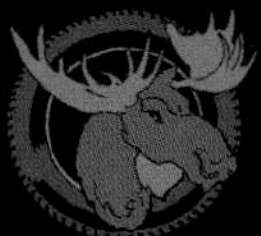

## MICHIGAN

Megafauna and other animals from the Great Lakes invaded and seized the means of production of vehicles. While all cars currently in circulation are still functioning, at least until the final consumption of the remaining oil and gasoline, the Animals are currently engaged in the creation of new armored vehicles designed for their own purposes. Production has already begun.

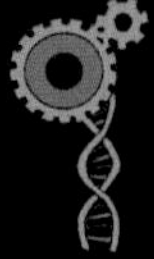

## MINNESOTA

Humans valiantly defended [illegible] factories and industries, winning in some places, losing in others, and striking tense bargains for the Animals to use the machines for their own purposes in exchange for Animal-made goods (whether wool, honey, milk, eggs or the flesh of those who had been killed or died of natural causes). Elsewhere, a laboratory deeply invested in biomedical engineering tries desperately to discover the cause—and perhaps cure—of the Wake.

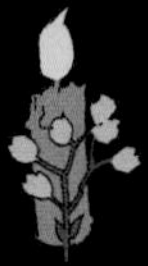

## MISSISSIPPI

The site of a dark and mysterious act of grace where Animals came from their fields, slow and silent, and walked up to the trembling humans, some armed, who awaited them. Some Animals knelt. Some lay their heads in the laps of the people who had cared for them. Even those who had done evil to their Animals were offered a chance at forgiveness. Those who did not surrender to this act of grace were turned upon and attacked and viciously slain—not by the Animals, but by the forgiven humans, who fell soon after to weeping and a grief so deep, they often never recovered.

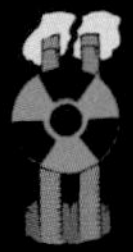

## MISSOURI

The site of a nuclear silo and stockpile, humans and Animals raced to keep the deadly weaponry from one another's hands and paws. A savage, barbaric siege took place, but humans and Animals worked together to overthrow a third combined force comprised of those who desired to trigger the missiles and end this mad new world.

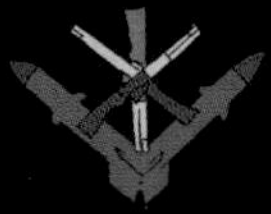

## MONTANA

As a state with one of the lowest human population densities, one of the highest gun ownerships, and one of the highest shooting incident reports, Montana remains an intense survival zone. Denizens live with only individual truces in a sometimes peaceful, sometimes bloody free-for-all.

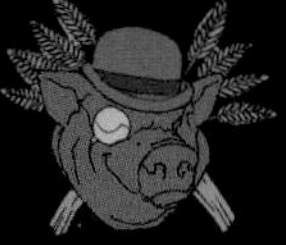

## NEBRASKA

The large population of swine attempted a political coup with the goal of integrating Animals into the human systems and society already in place. The hogs—insisting that their intelligence before the Wake guaranteed them increased intelligence after the Wake—negotiated with humans to extend political rights to Animals, though their Orwellian motives were fairly predictable in the end. The state is marked for annexation by the Horse Lords, particularly by the warlike stallion Tencendor.

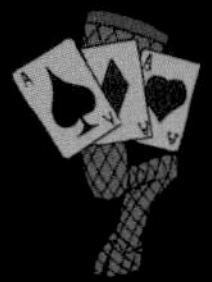

## NEVADA

One of the strangest territories, Nevada is now host to those who wish to spend their final days in hedonism. Few acts of revenge took place during the Wake, with most creatures—both human and Animal—giving themselves up to debauchery amid the violence of the day. The human/Animal sex trade thrives in the overgrown and crumbling ruins of the former hotels and casinos, and is self-regulated by squads and gangs protecting the interests of their own. Elsewhere, cultists gather in the desert, certain that alien intervention caused the Wake and attempting passionately to make contact with supposed visitors from another world.

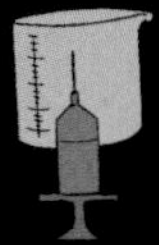

## NEW HAMPSHIRE

The site of an underground laboratory and bunker engaged in intense and unethical experimentation on post-Wake Animals. Humans and Animals alike are hunting for it to free those within—and harvest whatever information they may have gathered.

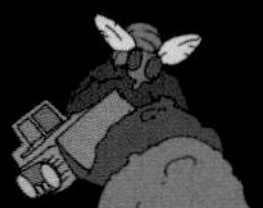

## NEW JERSEY

Hordes of Animals began unearthing the landfills, sorting, cleaning, dividing, trading and s[redacted] the salvage. The task is far less repuls[redacted]nimals, many of whom are used to scavenging or already dwell in the landfill. The collection of plastics, electronics and machinery is now precious, given the trade agreements, the production of energy and manufacturing which have now come to a screeching halt.

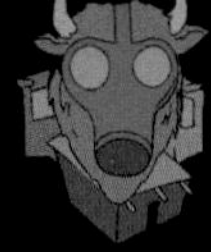

## NEW MEXICO

Home of the Los Alamos Lab, studying everything from the origins of the Wake, to plagues deadly to both humans and Animals, to futuristic superweapons. The state is contested territory currently under expansion by Native tribes imprisoned for decades on dwindling reservations, aided by Animals keen to overthrow the remains of the American authorities still in the area.

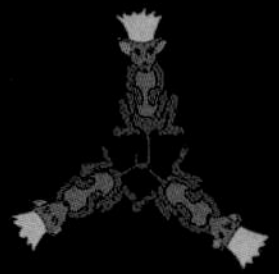

## NEW YORK

The Three Princes of New York—together, known as the Rat King—rule the sewers of New York City. Manhattan is an isolated city, and entrance or exit is forbidden and punishable by death and devouring. The rat population has exploded post-Wake, and they use their human citizens to maintain the city. Life is neither so good nor so terrible, and each remaining human and Animal has their duties in this dystopia. Art, Literature, science and education thrive despite the tyranny of the rats. A strange, jagged new society is emerging.

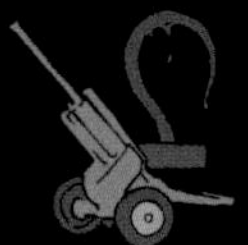

## NORTH CAROLINA

The site of the largest slaughterhouse in America, North Carolina was home to horrific violence long before the Wake. The livestock within led a dreadful and terrible uprising, helmed by a black heifer who was born with a number instead of a name. "The Maiden," as she is now known, is a herald and prophetess to her people, who are engaged in a staggering and Biblical rebellion.

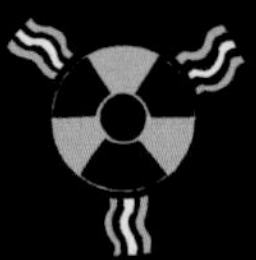

## NORTH DAKOTA

The location of a nuclear silo, and a state surrounded in much mystery. Something terrible happened here within twenty-four hours of the Wake, and the nuclear facility poisoned much of the surroundin[redacted]. An explosion? A meltdown? The detai[redacted] participants are unknown, and no one h[redacted] to go anywhere near this territory any longer. Insects and birds exposed to even strong breezes die quickly, and human beings suffer rashes, bleeding and radiation poisoning the closer to the site they

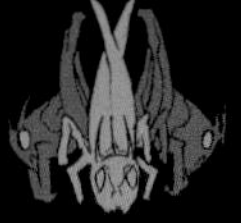

## OHIO

A horde of insects, swarms dense enough to blacken the sky, swept through the agricultural territory of Ohio. Grasshoppers, crickets, beetles, cockroaches, butterflies, etc. met as if in a terrible summit, and stripped every shred of green from the fields and forests. The super-horde moved unpredictably through the country, a plague out of the End Times, devouring all food they come across.

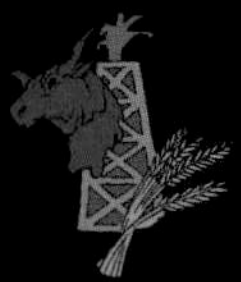

## OKLAHOMA

The site of a failed Animal uprising. Humans maintain much control of the precious oil fields, working with Animal mercenaries, but their hold is tenuous, and their food supplies were poisoned by Animal conspirators. The Horse Lords plan to seize this territory as well, under the military command of the ruthless mare Matsukaze.

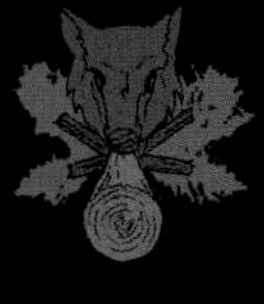

## OREGON

Many Animals retreated to the[redacted]orests to establish separatist communities, [redacted]d live in the mist and pines there, haunted by ghostly specters. Small societies have sprung up in the trees, especially the Lupercal, the largest orphanage in the known world. Here, Animal communities work together to provide for the children—human and Animal alike—orphaned in the Wake. All are raised as Animals, and trade lumber and labor to the humans in exchange for goods.

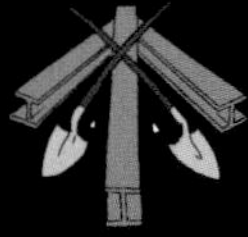

## PENNSYLVANIA

Humans and Animals alike labor in the mines and mills for resources, which they trade to forces and factions in other states. The new society is squalid and often viol[redacted]ith hunger-driven conflicts on both sides, [redacted]e clannish communities provide for their [redacted] first and their neighbors second, and ferociously defend those of their own territories above anyone from outside the state. The deer alone are saboteurs, viciously killing any human they come across.

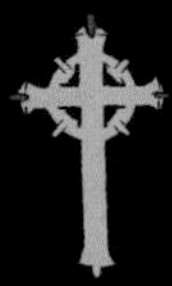

## RHODE ISLAND

The Archdiocese of Rhode Island declared Animals to be rational beings with souls, capable of sin and salvation, who will enter heaven or hell depending on their actions on Earth. This pronouncement swelled the ranks of the Church with Animal soldiers willing to defend them, outraged human believers over the audacity of the declaration, and was also met with sublime indifference by many other Animals who ate their way through the pantries of several local churches.

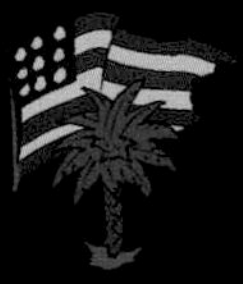

## SOUTH CAROLINA

The new Capital of the United States, and retreat of the last of the American leaders. Many American heads of state fell during the Wake, from the rogue bald eagle who took down Air Force One to the Mad Million, several allied colonies of ants that burrowed, infiltrated, sabotaged and detonated a bunker housing many human world leaders. The functional remains of the United States government are protected by General Nyota Gutiérrez, the highest-ranking officer among those who escaped the firebombing of the White House.

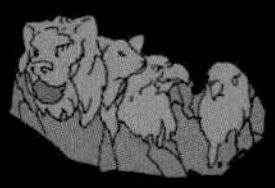

## SOUTH DAKOTA

Some ultimately very rude graffiti that probably wasn't an incredibly good use of someone's time during the apocalypse.

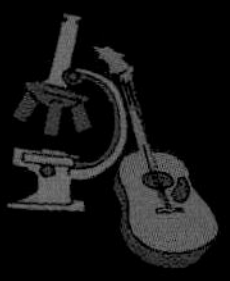

## TENNESSEE

Home of the Oak Ridge National Laboratory, where human and Animal scientists are tentatively working together to study the Wake, under the assurance that this laboratory will in no way try to control, reverse, or attempt to cure it. Much of the Wake defies scientific explanation, especially the Animal's ability to speak without the existence of vocal cords designed for that purpose. Some Animals rumored to speak do not have brains, but these cases have not yet been proven. It is also the site of some sweet country music, if you're looking to drink yourself through the End Times.

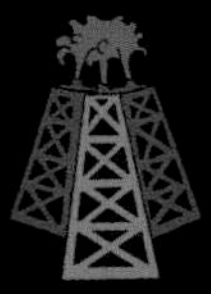

## TEXAS

Texas has split into several oil kingdoms, where barons rule vast swathes of territory, complete with armed human knights and peasant livestock who work the land. The kings of Texas operate as if they are countries unto themselves; living and dying brutally in the vast grasslands and deserts, and trading or selling supplies to all visitors. Survivalists are having a blast. Those caught in the middle, human and Animal alike, less so.

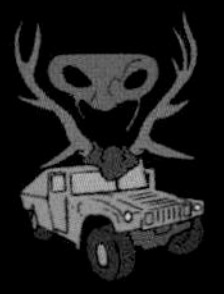

## UTAH

The site of a lingering pocket of the US Military desperately trying to reunite with command. The Mormons, who got to feel pretty swell for being the first among the Christian faiths to declare that Animals have souls, were largely left undisturbed. However, a massive population of pets and domestic animals turned on owners that they had witnessed being abusive to those dependent on them. The remaining families were treated quite well by the post-Wake Animals, and adopted into Animal clans who provided for them with great loyalty. However, a splinter cell of Animals went into the mountains, believing themselves now to be the final and most favored children of God, and no one is entirely sure what they are doing out in the wilds.

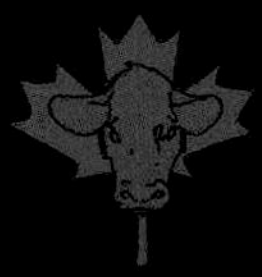

## VERMONT

Site of the House of Red Clover, the first formal school for the Animals. Led by Sugar Maple, a former dairy cow, and taught by senior Animals pooling their accumulated knowledge, the school is aided by human allies. Class sizes number in the hundreds to thousands as the Animals are taught languages, writing, mathematics, technical skills, history, science and technology heretofore unknown to them.

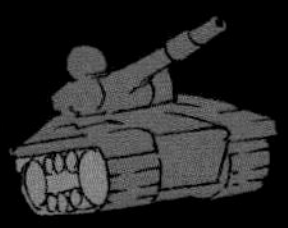

## VIRGINIA

The site of Hourglass Falls, a safe haven where many humans and Animals have passed to rest, or to peacefully end their lives. Virginia was also the location of a massive military and naval force, particularly in Norfolk, where many American battleships were stationed. The Virginia branches of the military—including some Animal allies—were essential in ushering the remains of the United States government through a 500-mile battle zone to South Carolina, where they were able to regroup in a secret fortress.

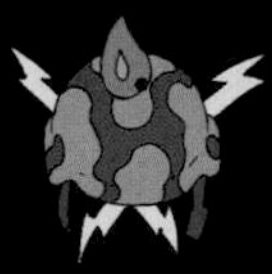

## WASHINGTON

On the night of the Wake, in a pouring rainstorm, human engineers and workers united to protect the plants and dams from enraged Animals seeking to disrupt and destroy human supremacy. The humans were outnumbered, ten-to-one in biomass alone, when they were joined by massive flocks, herds, schools and swarms of Animals seeking to protect the source of the electricity, which they felt essential to the protection of Animal-kind and the function of a new and peaceful society. The immense battle—during which some plants fell in dazzling explosions of electricity through the flooded areas, leading to devastating electrocutions and blasts that lit up the sky—ended in a victory for the humans and their Animal rescuers, who attempted to maintain the power for both human and Animal benefit.

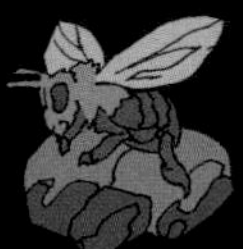

## WEST VIRGINIA

The Animals work in the mines alongside humans to bring up the coal, which they trade for resources from other states. Treachery and cannibalism are not unheard of, but the clannishness of the communities prioritizes those of one's own family and township above even one's species. Communities act ruthlessly with one another, but are sternly protective of their own.

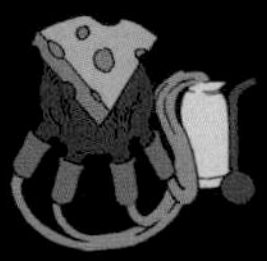

## WISCONSIN

A hub of the dairy industry, and site of some of the cruelest and most vile discoveries both before and after the Wake. What happened here is not spoken of by either humans or Animals.

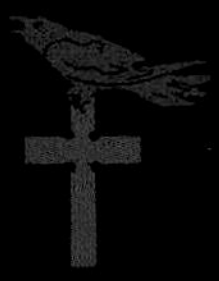

## WYOMING

Allied flocks of birds, turning on other species, claimed huge parts of this territory for themselves, and they have managed to keep it. They have begun to construct a humanoid society all their own, complete with garments, songs, customs, and massive structures to which they contribute. Ground-dwelling Animals respond with human weaponry and poisoned corn, but the Nation of the Birds will undoubtedly become a terrible and efficient power in the near future. Also the site of a small cult that believes this to be the end of days, though they are not above doing occasional labor for the birds in exchange for food.

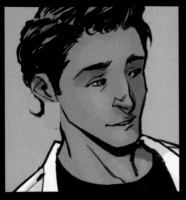

## ADAM NORTH

**Species:** Human *(Homo sapiens)*

**Age:** 29 years of expected 78 years

**Location Born:** Boston, Massachusetts

**Vorous:** Omnivore

**Weight:** 180 lbs

**Height:** 6′1″

**Profile:**

Insecure, anxious, and always longing to do the right thing, Adam North is one of the precious few veterinarians remaining to San Francisco. Jesse's estranged half-brother, he is unaware of her journey to his door. He struggles to find—and dedicate himself to—the ultimate good in any situation. He fears doing harm.

Adam feels divided, unable to fit into any home, family or community. He has thought, at times, that his identity—bisexual, biracial and estranged from his mother, half-sister and stepfather—contributed to this feeling of alienation, but he worries that however or whenever he was born, he would still struggle to fit in.

He often preferred the company of animals because of the simplicity and honesty of their emotions, of their indifference to the fact that he was unlike them—they merely loved him, without ever expecting him to be like them.

He feels particular regret for the breakdown of his relationship with his mother, Shannon, after the death of his father, Micah, who lost his battle with cancer when Adam was ten. His half-sister, Jesse, is a total stranger to him.

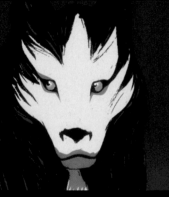

## WINTERMUTE

**Species:** Wolf-Malamute hybrid *(Canis lupus x Canis lupus familiaris)*

**Age:** [redacted]

**Location Born:** [redacted]

**Vorous:** [redacted]

**Weight:** 110 lbs

**Height:** 2′5″

**Profile:**

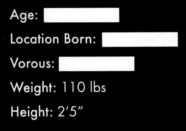

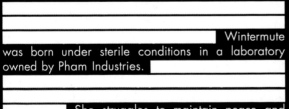

[redacted] Wintermute was born under sterile conditions in a laboratory owned by Pham Industries. [redacted] She struggles to maintain peace and prosperity for Animal and human alike in the City by the Sea.

# BETHESDA

**Species:** American Bison *(Bison bison)*
**Age:** 10 years of expected 25 years
**Location Born:** Bethesda, Maryland
**Vorous:** Herbivore
**Weight:** 1,100 lbs
**Height:** 5'9"

## Profile:

Beth can't help the evil that was done to her before and after the Wake, but she has resolved not to let it take root in her heart. Her resilience and kindness are often taken for granted. Beth cares for and looks after others, but only Pallas understands that Beth, too, needs care and looking after.

Beth—known in turn as Bethesda, Bessie, Bette, etc. as she struggles to affix her identity in an often shifting world—is particularly affectionate to children and other small, lost, troubled things. She fears she cares for these creatures because she cannot care for her own calves, born in charitable captivity and taken to various nature preserves Lord knows where.

While Beth feels she has been fortunate—she was

born a bison, not a dairy cow or head of cattle—she struggles with the idea that she should be grateful for her position. She longs to be reunited with her lost children, but was thwarted in her search and the trail has since gone cold. Despite and because of her considerable size and strength, she is a prime target for hunters, scavengers and meat-eaters. She is safest with a group, and feels adrift without a family or herd around her.

Bethesda intends to help Jesse to San Francisco out of the hope that the Animals there—reputed to have built a massive, functioning society with advanced technology—will be able to help her find her lost calves. She is kind and loyal until provoked, and wants for her loved ones simply to be happy.

# PALLAS

**Species:** Pallas's cat *(Otocolobus manul)*
**Age:** Unknown years of expected 11 years
**Location Born:** The Himalayan Plateau
**Vorous:** Carnivore
**Weight:** 8 lbs
**Height:** 2'1"

## Profile:

Pallas was born in the steppes of the Himalayan Plateau, and lived a largely solitary life, occasionally outsmarting hunters amidst the wilds. Eventually, they were poached and brought to a laboratory as a test animal in an experiment to study the immune systems of various mammals when exposed to different diseases. Pallas's cats—also known as manuls—have notoriously poor immune systems, as they live at such intense heights where few viruses survive.

After the Wake, Pallas remained in the laboratory, studying the medical texts and interacting with the surviving scientists, doctors and veterinarians. Their keen intelligence and prodigious memory aided their education, though they are hindered by the limits

of human technology designed for human hands. Pallas served as a doctor and medic to the Animilitary, the White Wings, and other forces during and after the Wake. Pallas's main focus is the alleviation of pain and the prevention of harm.

Pallas is genderqueer, and is indifferent to the distinctions that humans make regarding the roles assigned to and expected of various genders. They are calm, thoughtful, intelligent and reasonably sympathetic to others. They have begun to develop a deep attachment to Beth, and consequently only express any sudden or excessive emotion when Beth is threatened or unhappy.

# KYLE KHAHN

**Species:** Human *(Homo sapiens)*

**Age:** 26 years of expected 78 years

**Location Born:** Unknown

**Vorous:** Vegan

**Weight:** 164 lbs

**Height:** 5'11"

## Profile:

Kyle was a Computer Science student who was expelled from several universities before the coming of the Wake. He was employed in the kitchens and cafeterias of the majority of the schools as part of a work/study program, as well as in several Brooklyn restaurants. His family situation is unknown.

Kyle has always struggled to live his life ethnically— abstaining from meat, from products created in sweatshops, from attending events in venues built by slave labor, etc. Others resented his efforts as performative and accused him of evangelization.

Kyle turned himself over to the creatures who would later become the Animilitary within days of the Wake, and served them faithfully until the coup by the American military and dissidents within the Animilitary's ranks. He felt it was the right thing to do.

When speaking to Jesse, Kyle alleges that he read her parents' case history in a file while working for the Animilitary, when in fact, Kyle discovered the bodies of Jesse's parents in New York City while he was there on a scavenging mission for Mimico, the Animilitary's leader.

Kyle struggles to maintain his sympathy for others when they do not return it.

# KEEKIRIKEE

**Species:** Giant golden-crowned flying fox *(Acerodon jubatus)*

**Age:** 3 years of expected 15 years

**Location Born:** Maitum, Sarangani, Philippines

**Vorous:** Frugivore

**Weight:** 2.5 lbs

**Wingspan:** 5'5"

## Profile:

Keekirikee came from the Philippines on a shipping freighter containing fresh mangoes and pineapples. As a stowaway entering to a new land, she escaped and hid out with flocks of bats along the California coast, preying on the orchards of inland farmers. Her native colony of bats numbered in the hundreds of thousands, and her new colony held around twenty thousand.

Moody and secretive, swaying between sudden intense cravings for affection or intensely despising those around her, Keekirikee is a creature of contradictions. She works as the primary guardian animal and chaperone of Adam North in San Francisco, and she seems at a loss as to whether she would prefer many friends and family or none at all.

Keekirikee resents that the Wake brought human awareness—and the burden of human sadness—into her life. She often considers that she was happier as a mere fruit bat, and though she knows the gift of her cognizance is just that—a gift—she struggles with feeling ungrateful. She envies humans for their ability to cope with sentience, and enjoys human hobbies, like swimming, and human jewelry and clothing. She is prone to outbursts of sudden teasing, flirting and jokes, but follows them just as suddenly with icy silence. She wishes she were happier, but doesn't know what would give her life meaning.

# SHANNON MANDEL

**Species:** Human *(Homo sapiens)*

**Age:** 40 years at time of death

**Location Born:** Boston, Massachusetts

**Vorous:** Omnivore

**Weight:** 132 lbs

**Height:** 5'6"

## Profile:

The only daughter of an old family, and a noted physicist in her own right, Shannon lived the majority of her life in great loneliness. She was an exemplary student, a debutante and pioneer in her field, but often felt hollow—was this all there was to life?

At twenty-five, she married the novelist Micah North, who she felt understood her fears, and for a few years, she, Micah and their son Adam were very happy. When Micah was diagnosed and ultimately lost his battle with cancer, Shannon was devastated and sank into a profound depression. Years later, she would be tempted from her gloom by a charming literature teacher, Óscar Hernadez, who she met at a reading of one of Micah's posthumous collections.

After her wedding to Óscar and their whirlwind honeymoon, Shannon suffered from post-partum depression and feared being unable to bond with her newborn daughter, Jesse. This grief magnified through the increasing rejections of Adam, who never forgave her for remarrying five years after the death of his father.

Shannon often wondered if much of her life was a mistake, and during her days working at home, she confided—sometimes over a glass of wine—in the family dog, Sandor, who could not understand. This dog, on the day of the Wake, would recollect her years of loneliness, unhappiness, and confession with sympathy.

# ÓSCAR HERNANDEZ

**Species:** Human *(Homo sapiens)*

**Age:** 39 years at time of death

**Location Born:** Queens, New York City

**Vorous:** Omnivore

**Weight:** 159 lbs

**Height:** 5'10"

## Profile:

A mechanic turned high school literature teacher turned award-winning college professor, Óscar was immensely proud to be a self-made man. Separated from his own family through the foster system at a young age, and raised by various distant relatives in turn, the tumult of his childhood and youth gave Óscar a profound sense of what he longed for in a family. All of his achievements have been in service to his wife, Shannon, and their daughter, Jesse.

Loving but jealous, Óscar employed the very furthest extents of his power to give Jesse every kindness and advantage he could, from the best books, to the best schools, to the most enriching experiences, to a newborn puppy that he named Sandor after "the Hound,"

Sandor Clegane, in one of his favorite fantasy epics, *A Game of Thrones.*

Óscar endured a great deal of tension with the ghosts of Shannon's past, fueled by insecurities of never being good enough as a provider for his wife and child. He compared himself first to Micah North, Shannon's late husband, and then to Adam, Shannon and Micah's son. During the Wake, when Sandor became another competitive figure in Óscar's life, threatening the stability and safety of the family—and Óscar's place in it—tensions escalated to the point of explosion.

# THE REST OF

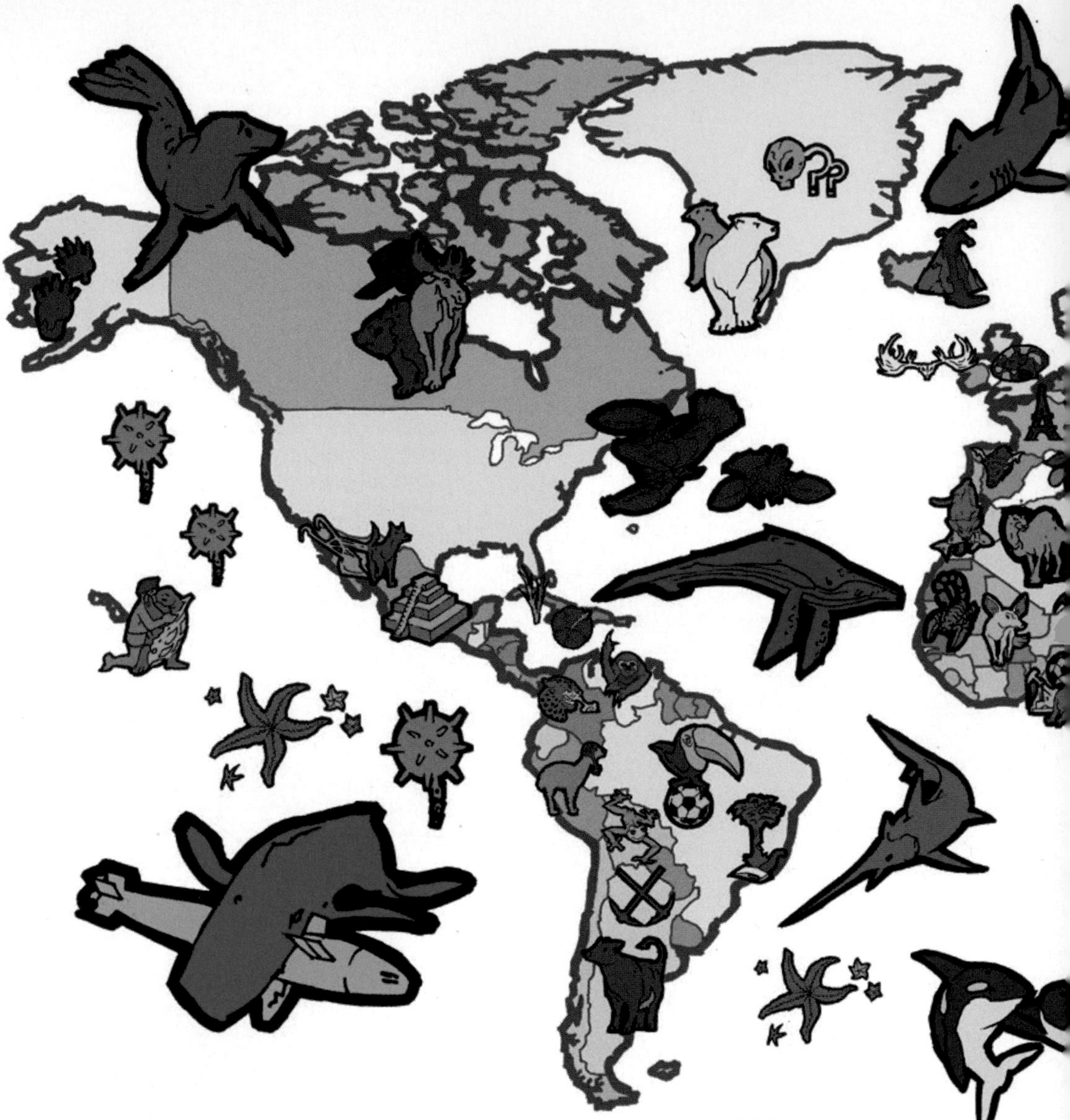

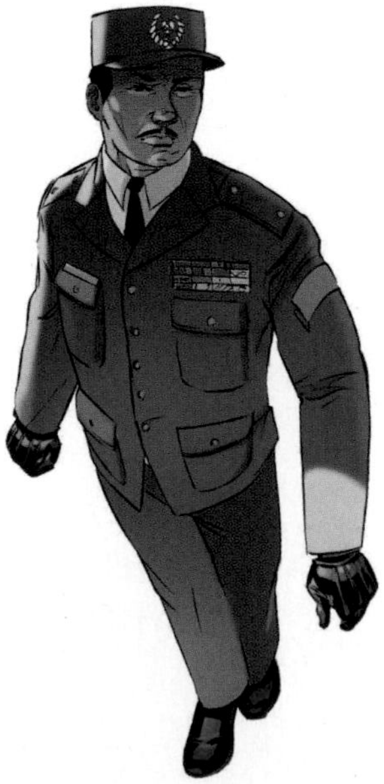

MAJOR DIEGO SINGH

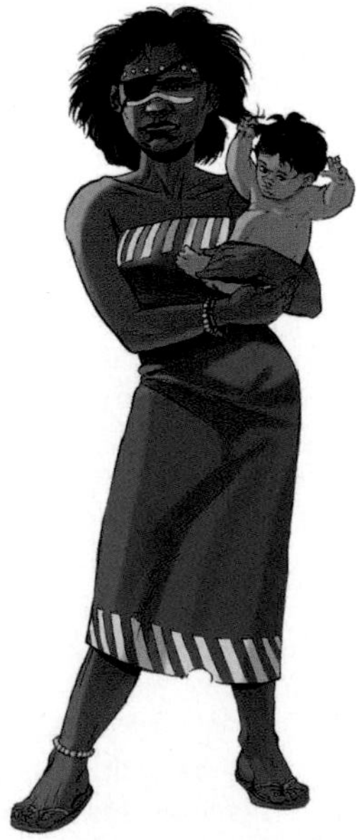

RUBY

# THE WORLD

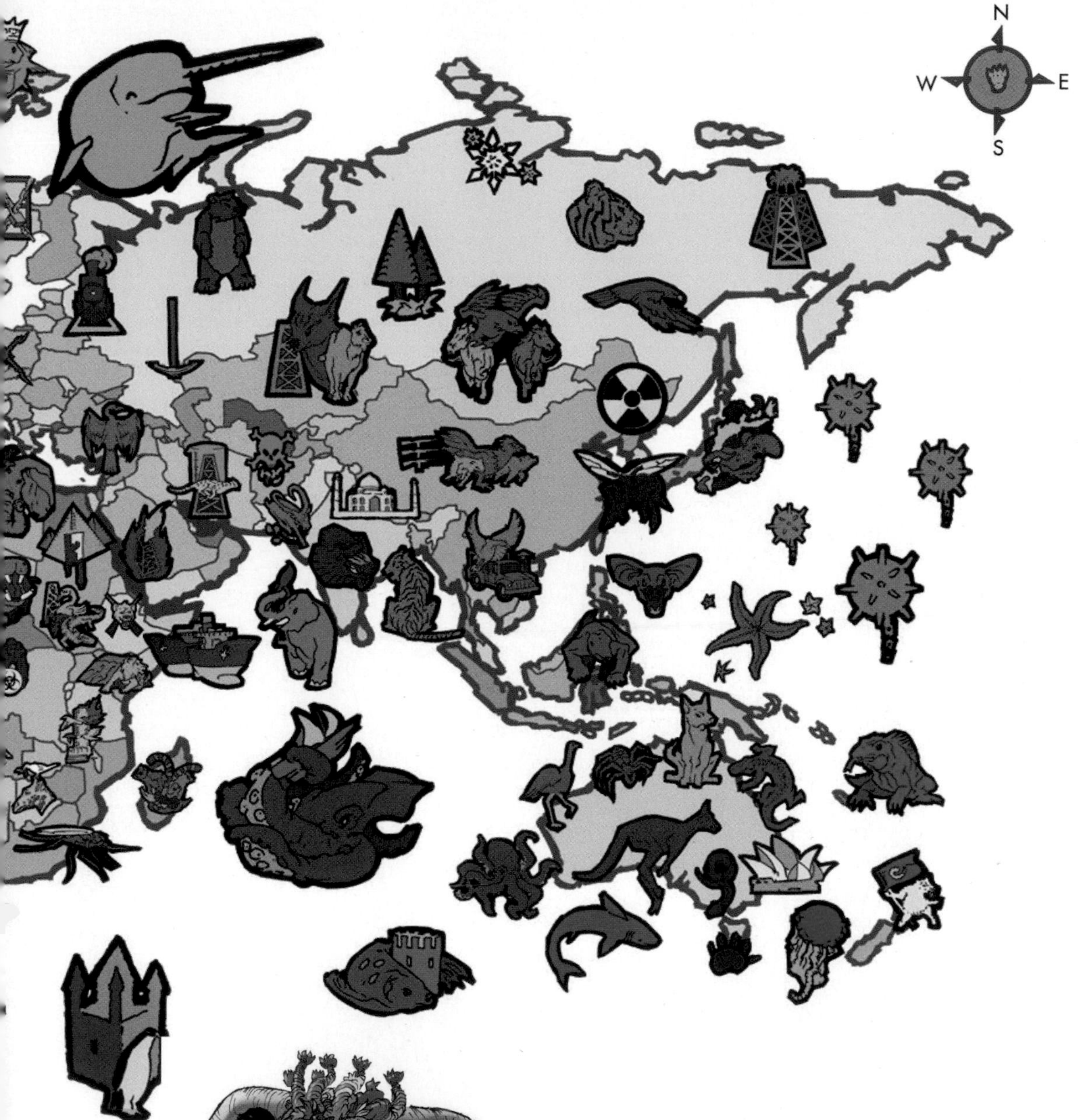
N
W
E
S

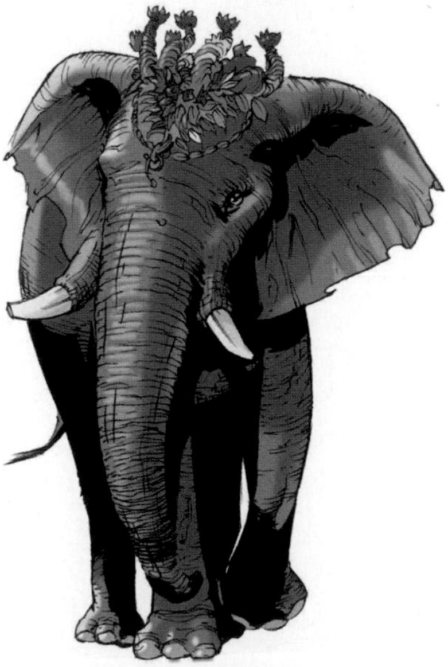

HASANA THE JUST

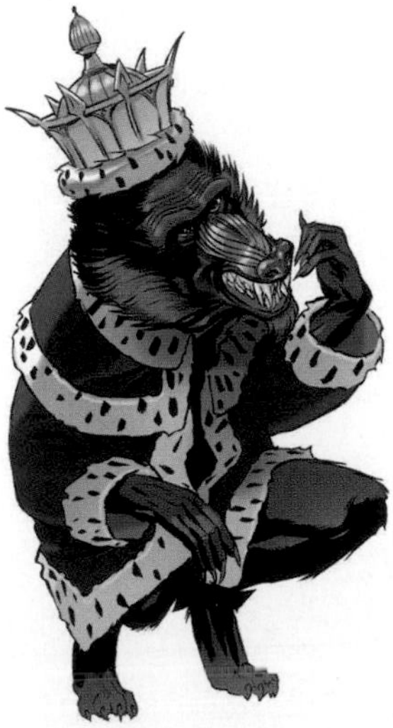

KING HAX

# AFRICA

## ALGERIA/LIBYA/MALI/MAURITANIA

This united territory is ruled by an elephant matriarch named Hasana who is advised and attended by a select council of humans and Animals alike. Hasana herself is revered as the symbolic grandmother of all the elephant herds in the upper two-thirds of the continent. She is the bitter, sworn enemy of the hyena matriarch Big Teeth, who killed her youngest grandcalf during a raid abetted by stolen motorcycles provided by Somali pirates. Animals of all species flocked to Hasana to protect her until she had amassed a mighty army, from the proudest lions to the smallest ants.

Hasana's campaign progressed through the nations of the north, quelling disputes and gathering new followers whom she fed, clothed and sheltered from predation. City by city, village by village, even humans swore her allegiance, and soon nearly the entire Animal population of the upper half of Africa pledged her their loyalty. She soon redistributed the land and resources for farming, setting Animals to solving crises of water, and settling hard disputes among families.

Unbeknownst to many of her loyal followers, but well known to her bitter enemies, is that Hasana has kept her power through the orchestration of a massive truce with the mosquitos of the continent. She offered her enemies and those cities unwilling to kneel as prey to the insects infected with malaria, while negotiating that those under her protection were to be spared the dreaded sickness. Her devotees call her "Queen Solomon," and her enemies call her "The Bloody Trumpet."

## DEMOCRATIC REPUBLIC OF THE CONGO

Intense outbreaks of new zoonotic diseases carried by apes and monkeys reached critical peaks as Animals flooded from the jungles and into high-density human populations. Ebola, sleeping sickness and complications arising from mutations of HIV all poured forth with the exodus of the Animals.

## EGYPT

The site of a notoriously bloody riot in Cairo as livestock stampeded out of meat markets, killing hundreds, and were gunned down by soldiers. Cairo arranged a mass extermination of all Animals thought to be "infected," though many families hid their beloved pets or smuggled them outside of city limits. Animals claiming to be gods or the avatars of long-dead pharaohs seized upon Ancient Egyptian mythology, and devotees flocked to their numbers, while the crocodiles took control of the Nile and threatened to poison sources of fresh water if Animal demands are not met.

## ETHIOPIA

The hyena called Big Teeth, a military matriarch, is head of a counsel of humans and Animals, governing a "pack" of three hundred thousand souls as raiders in a mobile camp over several hundred miles. Her reliance on technology, from tanks to torpedoes, makes her a formidable threat, but one whose *modus operandi* is as a reaver and raider with no plan for the future beyond survival.

## KENYA

A whole lot of lionesses murdered a whole lot of lions over the routine butchery of cubs to whom the sauntering male lions were not related. Less than 10% of the original number of adult male lions in the nation are left, while the lionesses formed nations of their own. One lioness, called the Scarred One, declared that humankind is safe from her people, so long as they leave huge swaths of territory and the national parks to the lions, and mind their own business in the cities. The herbivores were not invited to comment.

## MADASCGAR

One of the most biodiverse nations on Earth, with 90% of its wildlife occurring nowhere else on the planet, Madagascar is self-sustaining and largely having a party as it watches what the rest of the world plans to do.

## MOROCCO

Morocco has become a vast port city where people and Animals can trade and sell goods, or arrange secret travel on smugglers' ships, to any destination in the world.

## NAMIBIA

Antelopes, springboks, dik-diks, wildebeest, klipspringers, kudus, oryxes, gemboks, water buffalo, etc. murdered the absolute ever-loving shit out of tourism hunters and poachers, dragged the bodies to the border, and dumped them in South Africa.

## NIGERIA

The technological advances of Nigeria meant that it had more to lose in the Wake. Nigeria successfully maintained control of the nation, due in part to the extermination of rebel squads of Animals, but suffered some of the lowest loss of human life on the continent. Animals entered the major urban areas in droves, looking for food, care and explanations of their current state, and were housed on soccer fields and in sporting arenas until employment could be found for them.

## SENEGAL/GUINEA/COTE D'IVOIRE/ SIERRA LEONE/GHANA/BURKINA FASO

An enormous barricade, over a thousand miles long, was erected to separate Senegal, Guinea, Cote d'Ivoire, Sierra Leone, Ghana and Burkina Faso from the rest of the continent, though there are gaps in this massive defense system that are exploited by smugglers. The barricade, initially erected to prevent disease and the onrush of Animals and refugees alike from overwhelming the coast in mass starvation, has largely protected it. Land Animals and humans have formed alliances against the fish, and work together to hold off famine—but hoarding, betrayal and concealment of disease are strenuously punished.

## SOMALIA

Human pirates, aided now by sea birds and sea creatures, have become one of the most formidable forces on the seas. Certain Animals now helm their own ships in a huge pirate navy directed by a Captain Afrax and his bloodthirsty ostrich wife.

## SOUTH AFRICA

Humans in any form of power were expelled en masse from the country, some fleeing by plane and others by yacht, as the Animals burned large portions of the country to the ground, and seized food caches to redistribute among those remaining. Humans willing to fight with the Animals were spared and rewarded. Humans who fought for the leaders who were ejected were driven into the shallow water as gifts of alliance to the sharks.

# ANTARTICA

## ANTARTICA

The last unclaimed kingdom, all but devoid of humanity. Only a few thousand humans were present at scientific research stations during the Wake. Some became hostages, others became allies to the Animals, others attempted to flee, others attempted to do their scientific duties and study the events, and others were slain by warring clans of Animals attempting to seize human facilities (and in at least one case) human slaves. The continent is divided into warring clans of penguins attempting to seize power and ease the brutal struggles of their lives, while leopard seals and killer whales make devious alliances in the seas.

# ASIA

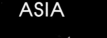

## AFGHANISTAN

The site of a dreaded outbreak of the smallpox. The bacteria, which had been considered extinct, was uncovered in an isolated village and carried in infected carrion by a vulture. Humanity, which no longer vaccinates against the disease, was unprepared, and the plague burned through huge swaths of the country. The world was in such chaos that little medical aid could be sent to stop the spread. Animals, immune to the smallpox strain, acted as guardians, liaisons, doctors and runners to acquire the vaccine for the humans left uninfected, and sit as caretakers of the dying and protectors of the living. This is one of the only known cases where the human nation was paralyzed, and relied on the kindness of the Animals for survival.

## CHINA

As the country with the largest population of humans in the world, so too did China have the largest population of livestock. The billions of cows, pigs, sheep, chickens and more rose up in a devastating civil war, sparking a massive famine and colossal conflict, leaving hundreds of millions dead.

## FIJI

With air travel collapsing on the day of the Wake, and the seas far too dangerous with vengeful ocean life, anyone on Fiji during the Wake is still on Fiji after the Wake. Animals and humans, after some initial bewilderment, are making the best of their environments, redistributing the wealth and resources, and many taking up housing in the luxury resorts. A pretty swell time, to be honest, especially since if anyone tries to take more than his fair share, you can feed him to the lizards.

## INDIA

Areas with the highest population density suffered intense violence as humans and Animals, in a panic, lashed out at one another—human against human, Animal against Animal, and everyone against each other in a desperate bid to protect their loved ones. Looting, burning and panic caused huge devastation in the most populated cities, and the military was unable to control any Animal populations without unforgivable costs to human life, and so did not fire upon any urban areas.

Power was seized by one Mandrill, the imported pet of a notorious gangster, who declared himself at first to be a king and then a god. The Mandrill, called Hax, seized control of huge caches of food and weaponry, and all lesser monkeys and apes swore fealty to him. He lives as a king in villas abandoned during the violence, and controls human populations through the threat of infection and disease and the seizing and raising of human infants to be his own soldiers.

In turn, an eight-year-old she-elephant calf called Tapani beseeched that the Animals and humans live peacefully, and led huge communities away from the cities to live in small farming villages where they might care for each other in accordance to their needs and abilities. The Animals and humans work the land as stably as possible, with Animals adopting human dress and custom, and attempt to stave off famine.

## INDONESIA

Fighting gamecocks exploded out of the ring, turning on many who had gathered to watch the bloodsport and declaring that the humans would now have to fight and die in gladiatorial combat for the pleasure of the roosters and their wives and chicks. Those in urban areas suffered most, usually due to panic, while those in more remote areas were able to swiftly orchestrate alliances with the Animals to protect their territory from those fleeing the cities. Komodo dragons have established themselves as pagan gods who raise armies of lizards to raid human villages, while the Animals of the faithful do their best to defend their humans and understand their own identities and roles in this brave new world.

## IRAN

n the chaos of the Wake, cities have isolated themselves, shutting their doors and attempting to survive in small, insulated units. In one such city, the University dominates the community, and one man, known as the Professor, tries to ethically explore and understand the nature of the Wake. His companion, in the small garden and courtyard of the library that is his domain, is a she-cheetah, with whom he discusses the philosophy of the world and the will of God. She will one day be the death of him, but he does not know that yet.

## IRAQ

In the power vacuum left by years of brutality and instability, the chaos of the Wake has largely triggered a free-for-all, with Animals seizing whatever they can and attempting to have a massive orgy of food, mating, fun and chaos before what is surely the end of the world. The so-called "Prince of Baghdad" is a golden jackal who had orchestrated a vast network of Animals (armed with luxury cars and automatic weapons) to trade oil stores for whatever they might desire.

## JAPAN

Besieged by sea Animals, Japan is targeted for its cache of experimental biotechnology, included advanced prosthetic and synthetic limbs intended to be attached to systems suffering from intense nerve damage. Animals loyal to the humans now fight back viciously to protect their loved ones, but the seas team with life and far outnumber those on land. Sea life carried in by mercenary birds or creeping up through canals and reservoirs hold scientists hostage, offering lesser creatures such as oysters, fish and urchins as food in exchange for the technology.

## KAZAKHSTAN

Animals, great or small, were immediately rounded up for extermination by the humans. Those who would swear loyalty and occupy their pre-Wake roles were allowed to return to them, though speaking is punished with death. Those who refused were culled. Separatist groups hide in the hills.

## MONGOLIA

Little has changed.

## NORTH KOREA

A meltdown of a malformed nuclear reactor has rendered the country utterly silent, though some civilian survivors have been rumored to have slipped over the borders, aided by wild Animals.

## PAKISTAN

Humans and Animals alike worked together to prevent the nuclear armaments of the country from falling into the hands of those who believed that the end of days had come. The massive civil war that ensued erased much of the leadership of the nation, while in the hills, wise creatures of every species gather to teach whoever would come and listen.

## THE PHILIPPINES

The Philippines were the epicenter for a massive outbreak of nipah virus carried by infected bats, causing hemorrhaging, respiratory failure, encephalitis and meningitis. The country has been sealed. Status unknown.

## SAUDI ARABIA

Human forces, beset by powerful Animal rebels, drove and lured many rampaging creatures onto the oil fields, where they set the fields themselves ablaze to shatter the Animal resistance.

## SOUTH KOREA

A dreaded swarm of Asian giant hornets, the largest and most vicious hornets in the world, coalesced upon the most densely populated cities, causing devastation to humans and Animals alike. The stings resulted in anaphylactic shock, cardiac arrest and organ failure, in addition to collisions caused by drivers and conductors swarmed by the insects. The hornets harvested everything that could be devoured or carried off, but many seemed to kill only for the sake of killing. Intense gas bombing of the cities drove the giant hornets into the countryside, where alliances between human and Animal populations—particularly birds—turned upon them.

## THAILAND/LAOS/CAMBODIA/VIETNAM

Humans and birds quickly established truces among themselves to defend against the grasping hands and paws of other Animals and other nations who might seize power during this crisis and vulnerability. Birds were granted rights above all other Animals, though individual alliances are made with domestic Animals such as oxen. Cats, for example, were employed by the state to keep down the population of vermin. Creatures assumed new duties, though some now had power, and others lived just as before, though now they were cognizant of the horror of their fate.

## TURKEY

Animals in urban areas were exterminated or driven out, leading to a food crisis. Non-human Animals were declared illegal, and forbidden in the nation. The country crumbled, expending resources on trying to protect its people from Animals, firing bullets at birds in the sky, seeding the ground with poison against insects. The only anti-Animal isolationist nation, it will be short-lived as winter draws near.

# AUSTRALIA

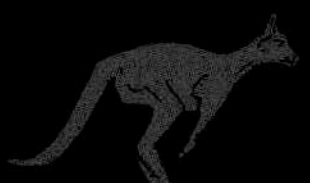

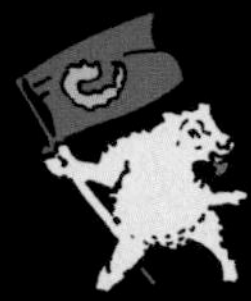

## AUSTRALIA

The deadly Animals of Australia may truly have met their match in the ferocity of its people, but the humans were too few. The detention centers (where imprisoned refugees were held for attempting to enter the country without documentation) were opened in the hopes of granting citizenship in exchange for taking up arms against the Animals. The Animals, who bowed only to the ancient peoples of the continent, sought the counsel of one named Ruby, a human woman who rose to usher in an uneasy end to the bloodshed. She beseeched the Animals to tear down the prisons that held the refugees, and with an army of the mightiest and deadliest creatures in the world at her back, offered all of the humans this alternative: live in peace, together, or die as invaders in a stolen land.

## NEW ZEALAND

Guess.

# EUROPE

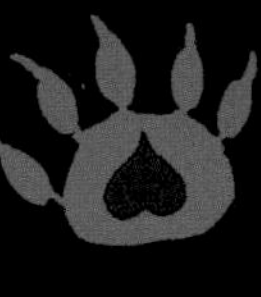

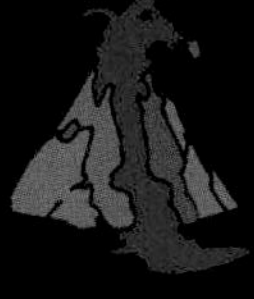

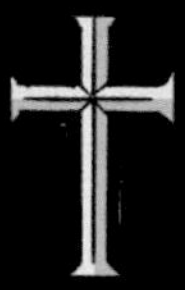

## EASTERN EUROPE

A vast survival zone, where strength, skill and the needs of one's family and community—whatever species that may be—triumph over all other considerations.

## FINLAND/NORWAY/SWEDEN

Believing the Wake to be caused by a plague or some other infectious origin, the Northern countries sealed their borders, and no human has gone in or out—though birds report the strangest tales of madness, occultism and heroism.

## FRANCE/GERMANY/POLAND

The intense bonds between humans and their domesticated Animals became a complex issue during the Wake. The humans displayed clear love for the Animals they kept as pets, while showing indifference or pleasantly enjoying the benefits of the deaths of Animals of other species. Many humans were executed under Animal law, while other Animals yet intervened on behalf of their humans. Some Animals were executed with their humans as traitors, and still others declare their love for one another and live as married couples. Chaos reigns, and town to town, community to community, often seem like separate worlds.

## ICELAND

Some believe the Wake was caused by ancient gods beneath the Earth, and have gone to find the gods and either thank or appease them.

## ITALY

The Pope was sealed within the Vatican for his protection, but is besieged on all sides by humans anticipating the end of days, and Animals begging for souls and the right to enter Heaven.

## RUSSIA

For Animals, speaking is punishable by death. Animal rebels coalesce in the hills and sewers, seeking a way to rebel and free their kin. Pre-Wake roles are rigidly enforced, and new livestock have their vocal cords removed at birth, though the full effect of this is not understood, as many Animals without vocal cords became capable of speech during the Wake. Whole human cities, when besieged by birds or insects, have elected to bomb themselves flat so long as the Animals go with them. Many human leaders have proven that they would rather go out as masters of the Earth than see themselves on equal footing with the Animals. The tigers to the East are seeking allies to rescue the remaining Animals under human control.

# NORTH AMERICA

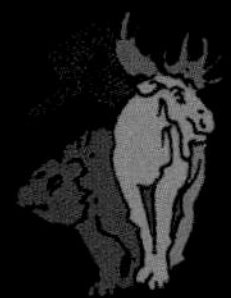

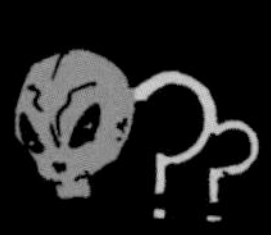

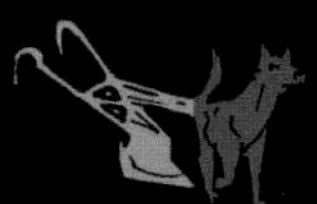

## CANADA

The Canadians fought well and honorably, but the Animals were far, far too many, and the moose, especially, fought dirty. The Animals keep the humans largely as pets and very indulged house servants. The country has one of the highest qualities of living in the world post-Wake, and Toronto alone has enough condos to house vast populations of Animals.

## GREENLAND

Home of the Greenland sharks, which live to be over 500 years old. The sharks are living libraries who gather students to whom they might tell the oral histories of the seas, lest the knowledge be lost forever. Also the site of where certain humans believe that extraterrestrials visited Earth in order to cause the Wake, though none of these theories have been verified.

## MEXICO

In urban areas with the most intense population density, immediate violence—human against Animal, Animal against human, human against human, and all species of Animal against one another—was explosive. The close quarters and immense claustrophobia of these environments led to 90% mortality in the worst cases, though this does not mean that mortality rate was equal among all species. After a week of incredible violence, the survivors emerged to a vastly altered landscape, and began to scavenge among the ruins.

In rural areas, however, the violence was dramatically decreased, and after the initial panic and chaos, family and community units did their best to stave off famine through working together, especially given that the initial violence had reduced the number of mouths to feed, and greatly increased the available arable land.

## UNITED STATES

Please see "The Former United States of America" section earlier in this issue.

# SOUTH AMERI[redacted]A

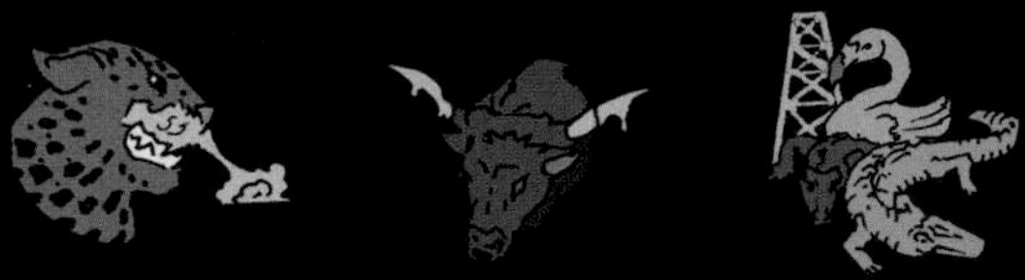

## ARGENTINA

Animal uprisings among cattle ranches were immense and enormously bloody, and Animal separatist nations were formed over the previous grazing land. The Cattle Land now permits select humans to enter their territory to perform actions that the livestock are unable to perform themselves, and in exchange, they offer those who have died of old age as meat.

## BOLIVIA

Humans will die if they enter the forest. That is the Animals' only law and request. If an Animal escapes to the forest, it will not be pursued. If an Animal escapes to the forest, humans may not pursue it. How the Animals rule among themselves is unknown.

## BRAZIL

The humans of Brazil put up one of the most spectacular civilian displays of power, holding back Animal forces for months after the Wake. The cities became battlegrounds as Animals flooded from the forests into urban areas, with humans up in high-rises, sniping with weaponry abandoned by the retreating army. Treachery plagued the factions, from humans going over to the Animals, wild Animals going over to the humans, and pets operating as heroic and conniving double agents to both sides.

The abandoned Olympic stadium was the site of a climactic and terrible battle, with flocks of parrots and toucans reigning down flaming torches from the sky, to swarms of insects blackening the atmosphere, to explosions of snakes writhing up from abandoned swimming pools. Both sides, mighty and exhausted, staggered to tense, uneasy truces that threaten at any moment to open again into total civil war.

## COLOMBIA

Animals have seized control of nearly all of the countries resources—natural, manufactured, legal and illegal, including the leopards, who have taken over the drug trade. Diego Singh, a major abruptly promoted through the ranks due to the immense violence during the initial week of the Wake, emerged as a force bent on restoring control to the country at any cost—so long as that control is a human control.

## CUBA

Large Animals and most mammals were immediately removed from the human population and taken to distant locations, where they were restrained and set to labor in agricultural fields. Human fatalities were few, but the birds and insects remain free, and are currently plotting a massive overthrow of the humans on the island.

## HAITI

Humans fleeing from other nations were welcomed to Haiti, so long as they abided by Animal law. Animals require humans to operate machinery designed for human needs, and threw themselves into agricultural endeavors at the expense of all else, determined that the island would not starve. Religious leaders, confounded as to the meaning of the Wake, initially believed it indicated the end of days, but revised to view the Animals as angelic messengers sent to aid the faithful and drive out human tyrants.

## SPAIN

After some initial bloodthirsty revenge, the Animals went off for a drink. Spain, exhausted, legalized pretty much everything and called it a day.

## SVALBARD

The kingdom of the fish. No one is really sure what's going on here.

## THE UNITED KINGDOM

This was the site of unspeakable chaos, from birds and insects tearing through London, shredding through skyscrapers until glass fell like rain, to waves of termites collapsing any and all wooden infrastructure in buildings, to explosions of gas and water lines sabotaged by vengeful rats and mice. Animals drove most humans from London, seizing the ruins for themselves, as humans fled from the city.

Foxes on horseback meticulously located, tracked and captured those who voted on the return of foxhunting. With hordes of [redacted]s beside them, they ran their prey to the ground, panting and bleeding. With their quarry surrounded, the foxes carefully brought forth one of their own number infected with rabies, bound in a straightjacket, frothing mad, and managed to use him with the utmost care. This infected fox was led to administer several bites to the captured party, who was then released into a forest guarded on all sides by the hounds, and left without treatment to die a very, very terrible death.

Humans with pets were largely defended by them, and survival came down to family units—those who foreswore eating meat, to those who would survive at any cost, to those who made plans about where they might go from here. Mother cats formed a network of communication through the cities and towns, striking deals with birds for information from abroad.

The entire world waits and watches and asks, "Where do we go from here?"

## VENEZUELA

Venezuela endured the total dissolution of its previous government, with Animals and humans alike uniting to drive out the remains of the former regime. The rebelling populace seized all factories and farmland, and is now desperately at work on how to offset famine with so many more mouths to feed. Animals proved most efficient at combating the military, as ants contaminated fuel storage and rodents destroyed interior machinery, rendering many vehicles useless, though armed soldiers managed to kill hundreds of thousands of both humans and Animals. The people are currently engaged in a massive rebellion—perhaps the only one where humans and Animals are allied against a common national enemy. Though famine looms, the country may be the first to reincorporate Animals into its laws when the nation is rebuilt.

A brave new world is coming.

We hope the **WORLD OF ANIMOSITY** one-shot was a fun and entertaining way to catch up on the epic world that Marguerite Bennett and Rafael De Latorre have created. For the full picture, be sure to pick up the first two trade collections:

MARGUERITE BENNETT · RAFAEL DE LATORRE
ANIMOSITY
VOLUME 1
THE WAKE

MARGUERITE BENNETT · RAFAEL DE LATORRE
ANIMOSITY
2
THE DRAGON

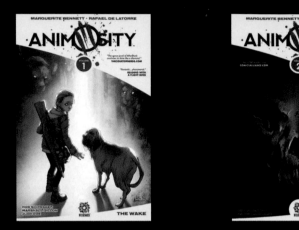

Also, don't miss out on the regular ongoing **ANIMOSITY** series...

MARGUERITE BENNETT · RAFAEL DE LATORRE #10
ANIMOSITY
ROB SCHWAGER · MARSHALL DILLON

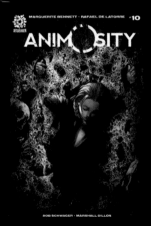

...and the special **ANIMOSITY: THE RISE** trilogy, which serves as a prelude to AfterShock's new regular series, **ANIMOSITY: EVOLUTION**, debuting in October!

ANIMOSITY
MARSHALL DILLON

MARGUERITE BENNETT · ERIC GAPSTUR #1
ANIMOSITY:
EVOLUTION
ROB SCHWAGER
MARSHALL DILLON

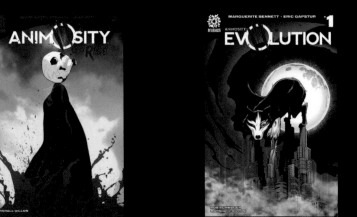

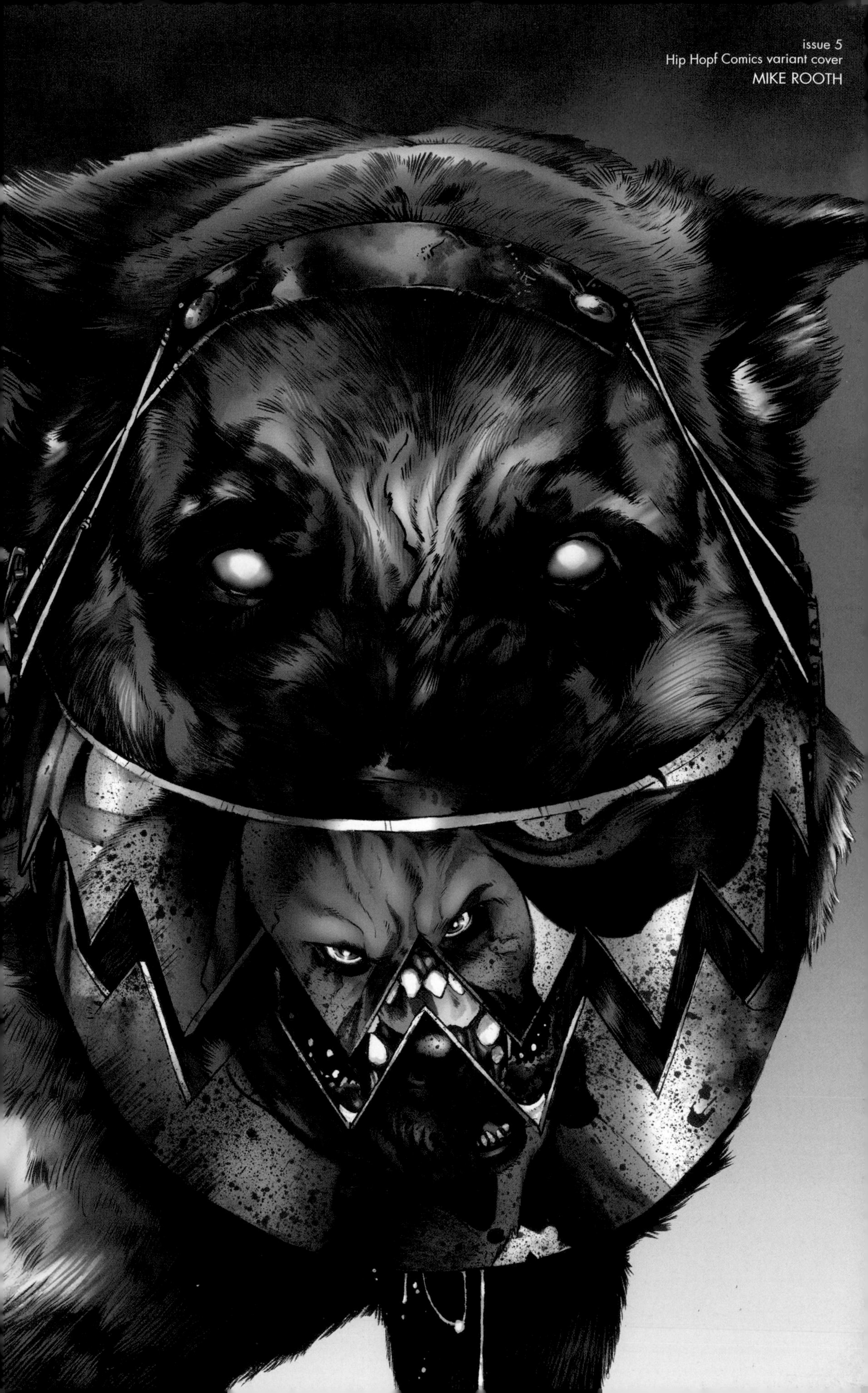

issue 5
Hip Hopf Comics variant cover
MIKE ROOTH

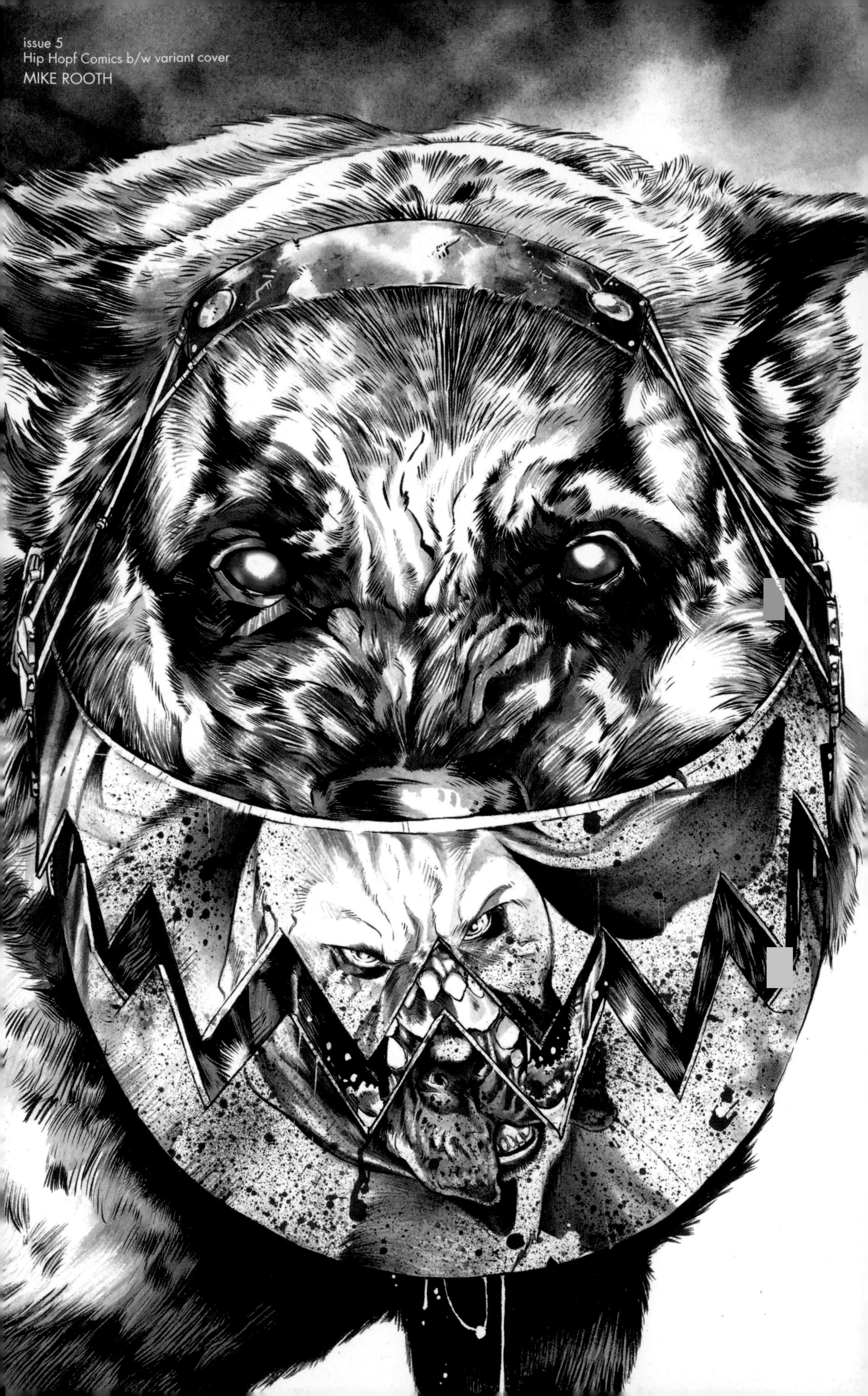

issue 5
Hip Hopf Comics b/w variant cover
MIKE ROOTH

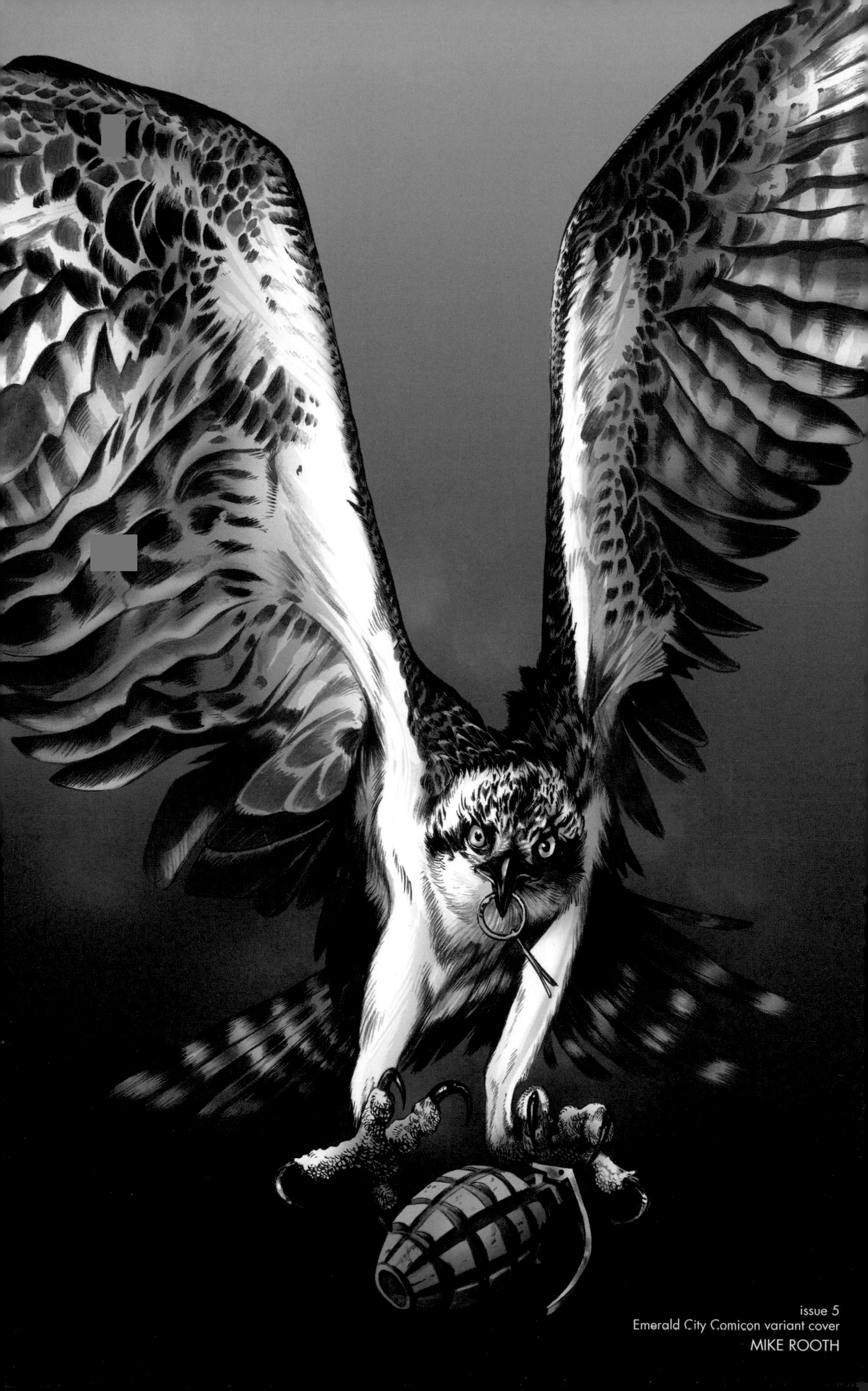

issue 5
Emerald City Comicon variant cover
MIKE ROOTH

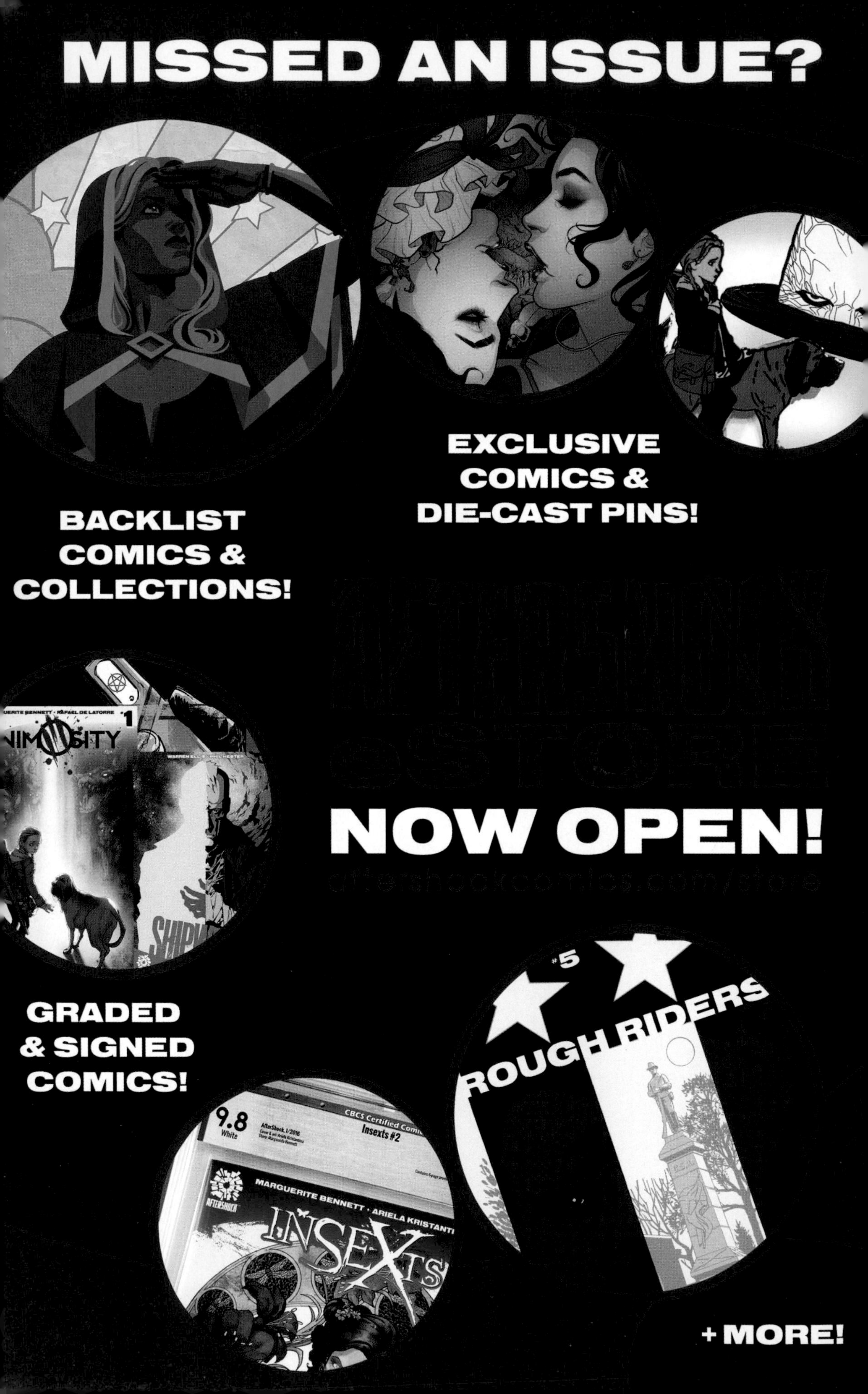

MISSED AN ISSUE?
EXCLUSIVE COMICS & DIE-CAST PINS!
BACKLIST COMICS & COLLECTIONS!
AFTERSHOCK
eSTORE
NOW OPEN!
aftershockcomics.com/store
GRADED & SIGNED COMICS!
ROUGH RIDERS
#5
9.8
White
CBCS Certified Comic
Insexts #2
MARGUERITE BENNETT · ARIELA KRISTANTINA
INSEXTS
+ MORE!

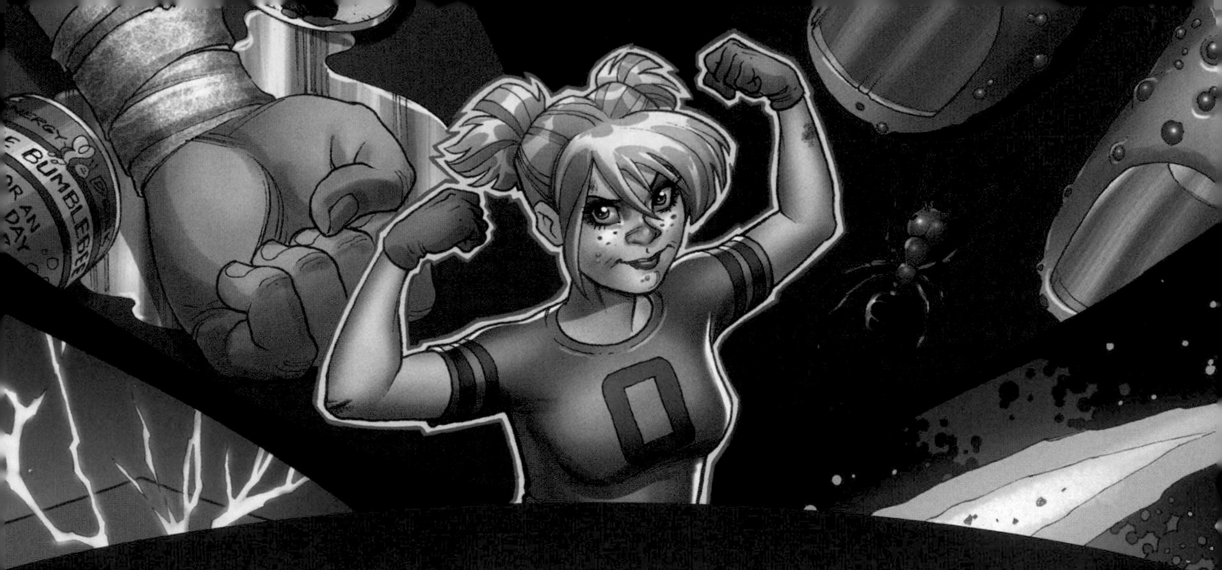
BUMBLEBEE

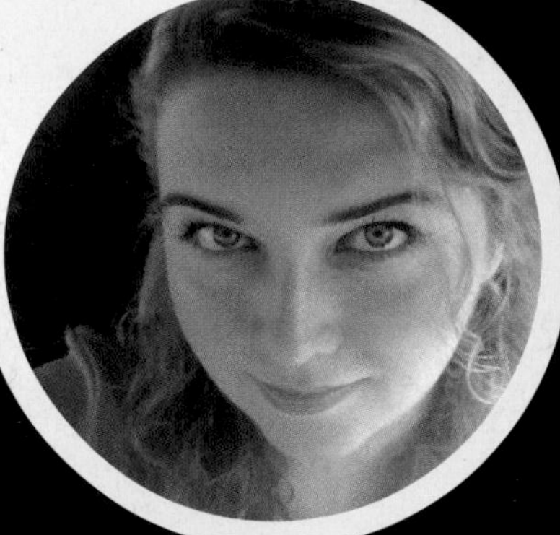

## MARGUERITE BENNETT writer

@EvilMarguerite

Marguerite Bennett is a comic book writer from Richmond, Virginia, who currently splits her time between Los Angeles and New York City. She received her MFA in Creative Writing from Sarah Lawrence College in 2013 and quickly went on to work for DC Comics, Marvel, BOOM! Studios, Dynamite and IDW on projects ranging from *Batman, Bombshells* and *A-Force* to *Angela: Asgard's Assassin, Red Sonja* and FOX TV's *Sleepy Hollow.*

## RAFAEL DE LATORRE artist

@De_Latorre

Rafael De Latorre is a Brazilian artist who has worked in illustration and advertising since 2006. His first comic book was *Fade Out: Painless Suicide,* which was nominated to the HQMix award in Brazil. He also worked on *Lost Kids: Seeking Samarkand* and *321: Fast Comics.*

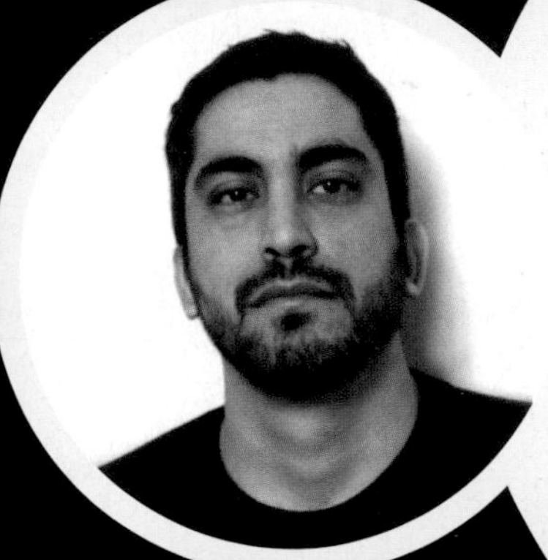

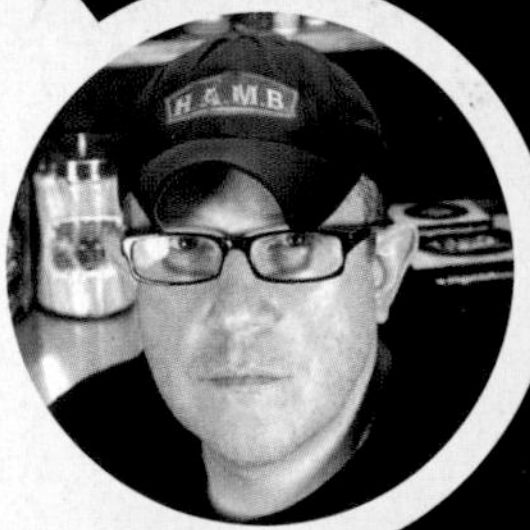
H.A.M.B.

## ROB SCHWAGER colorist

@robschwager

Rob Schwager is a self taught artist with over twenty-five years experience as a colorist in the comic book industry. He's worked on such iconic titles as *Batman, Superman, Green Lantern, Jonah Hex, Ghost Rider, Deadpool, Spider-Man, X-Men* and many others. He currently resides in the Tampa Bay area with his wife and three children and is extremely excited to be part of the AfterShock family of creators.

## MARSHALL DILLON letterer

@MarshallDillon

A comic book industry veteran, Marshall got his start in 1994, in the midst of the indy comic boom. Over the years, he's been everything from an independent self-published writer to an associate publisher working on properties like *G.I.Joe, Voltron* and *Street Fighter.* He's done just about everything except draw a comic book, and worked for just about every publisher except the "big two." Primarily a father and letterer these days, he also dabbles in old-school paper & dice RPG game design. You can catch up with Marshall at firstdraftpress.net.

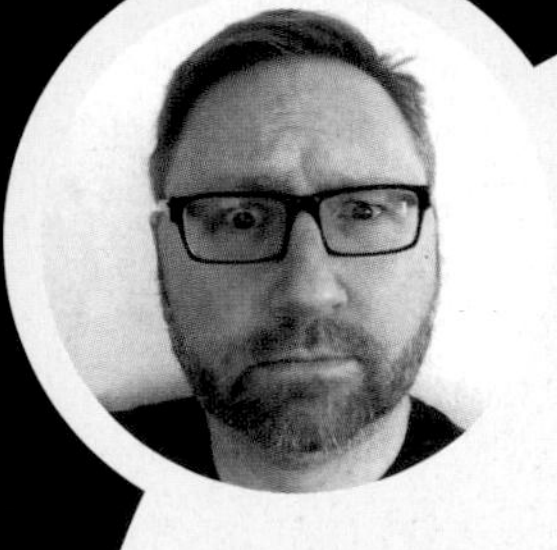